Becoming Ewe

A Woman's Journey from You to Ewe

RHONDA DE LA MORINIERE

WESTBOW
PRESS®
A DIVISION OF THOMAS NELSON
& ZONDERVAN

Scripture quotations are from The Holy Bible, English Standard Version® (ESV®), copyright © 2001 by Crossway, a publishing ministry of Good News Publishers. Used by permission. All rights reserved.

WestBow Press books may be ordered through booksellers or by contacting:

WestBow Press
A Division of Thomas Nelson & Zondervan
1663 Liberty Drive
Bloomington, IN 47403
www.westbowpress.com
1 (866) 928-1240

ISBN: 978-1-5127-1878-2 (sc)
ISBN: 978-1-5127-1879-9 (e)

Library of Congress Control Number: 2015918408

Print information available on the last page.

WestBow Press rev. date: 07/07/2016

To Mark Allen Lloyd and Emily Susan Hill (Mom &Dad),

Who could fathom the ways of God? It doesn't make sense that He would take a broken family, or a broken girl like me and create something beautiful and of substance. I love our family just as we are, lots of exclamation as well as question marks and that is okay. They have all led me to the One Who has answered my soul. I love you both and am thankful for your part in my becoming.

"He has made everything beautiful in its time. He has also set eternity in the human heart; yet no one can fathom what God has done from beginning to end." Ecclesiastes 3:11

Contents

Week 5 Becoming Ewe

INTRODUCTION

I wish I were with you right now, coffee cups and robes, bibles open, tissue-box near-by (just in case). Although I kind of know already, I would want to hear it in your own words, what brought you to this bible study?

There is a frustration that occurs when we become Christians and set out on our journey with Jesus. Bibles tucked in cute new bible bags, we tend to follow those other seasoned Christians along the path and soon wonder, "Where's the BEEF?" And then, like sheep, we lose interest and begin to wander.

And even when we have walked with Jesus for a while, there comes a time when we begin to wonder. "Am I really following You or just my idea of You?"

We can easily get stuck between wandering or wondering or both.

It is both the easiest and hardest thing in the world to truly follow the Good Shepherd. It is a process of BECOMING that can be compared to no other.

In this bible study, we will walk through the BECOMING together. We will take a view of Psalm 23 from a woman's point of view, and watch you become EWE right before our eyes.

I warn you in advance, just as the wolves come after the sheep in the world, they do in Spirit as well. I am praying for you, but you must pray for one another. If you are doing this study as part of a group, DON'T BE A STRAGGLER! They are the ones that get picked off first! If you are doing it alone, enlist someone to pray for you during this process. None of us Become Ewe alone.

One last thing, I encourage you to learn about sheep during this study. Ask Jesus to open your eyes to His truth about you and about Him. You will be AMAZED at how much He will speak to you about yourself as you learn about sheep. Two of the books I read as I prepared for this study are; Heaven Has Blue Carpet by Sharon Niedzinski and A Shepherd Looks at Psalm 23 by Phillip Keller. You will be so blessed if you give yourself a season to just take in ALL of what it truly means to be a follower of our LORD Jesus. There is SO much to learn from sheep!

You will get the most out of this study if you follow along with the videos that go along with the study. There is a video response page at the end of each week, as well as a few spots along the way called "Beside

Still Waters" that lead you to places to ponder more deeply what you are leaning about. The videos can be found for free at www.becomingewe.com or on youtube if you search for Becoming Ewe.

I am so honored and blessed to welcome you along on this journey. Soon we get to experience the weight of this worldly wool fall away from us as we realize that we never meant to carry any of the load alone. We have a faithful Shepherd, as well as a whole mess of other sheep to learn, laugh and grow with…all the way home.

His,

Rhonda de la Moriniere

Psalm 23

The LORD Is My Shepherd

A Psalm of David

1. The LORD is my shepherd; I shall not want.

2. He makes me lie down in green pastures. He leads me beside still waters.

3. He restores my soul. He leads me in paths of righteousness for his name's sake.

4. Even though I walk through the valley of the shadow of death, I will fear no evil, for you are with me; your rod and staff, they comfort me.

5. You prepare a table before me in the presence of my enemies, you anoint my head with oil; my cup overflows.

6. Surely goodness and mercy shall follow me all the days of my life, and I shall dwell in the house of the LORD forever.

He *MAKES Me Lie Down*

My guess is that, if you are doing this study right now, our beautiful Shepherd might just be *making you* lie down in green pastures. I am so happy that He has. Unfortunately, none of us are born with a natural bent towards following Our Shepherd. Just like lambs, He must teach us to do that.

One very interesting fact I learned in my study of sheep is that many lambs shed their coats during their first year of life on their own. There is no need for them to be subjected to that brutal experience of being tied down, helpless, believing that the end is drawing near, only to discover that life has suddenly become lighter, more wonderfully free from all the weight and parasites! Maybe that Shepherd isn't so bad after all!

I chuckled as I came upon this discovery. I am not sure where you are in your journey with the Shepherd, so I can only speak from my experience. As beautiful as my journey has been with my Shepherd, there have been times when I have been frustrated with Him that my wool has not *shed* as easily as it did in those years of walking with Him. Like a bird hovering over the nest of her newly hatched chicks, early on His grace hovered over me, kept me warm, fed, and taught me to trust Him and to feel safe in His Presence. My worldly wool began to fall away under His loving care. Then came the day when He began to nudge me out of the nest. I will never forget when He asked me to join a Sunday School class. This bird was scared to join the flock! Like Moses descending down the mountain to find the golden calf, I too had to discover that Jesus had come for sinners. And that they could be found in Sunday School class, with myself being chief among them.

I love knowing that, when we don't have the foresight or ability to do it, Jesus can and will, *"make us lie down in green pastures."* He will even use people in Sunday School to help do it (Did I tell you I met my husband in Sunday School?). Like a sheep before his shearers, we sometimes find ourselves in situations where we are completely constrained, where there is nowhere else to go or nothing else we can do.

These are Lying Down Moments.

We hate them at fist. But after they pass, they become some of the pin hole in our lives through which we can look through and see that heaven has opened up…just for us.

God moves when we rest. And often we won't rest until He makes us.

Psalm 46:10 says, *"Be still, and know that I am God; I will be exalted among the nations, I will be exalted in the earth."*

Despite us, our Shepherd knows when it is time…time for us to lie down so He can stand-up and Be God over us.

BECOMING EWE

O f all the animals in God's creation, He chose the weakest, most small-minded, timid and defenseless to characterize us, His children. Yet He calls us, His sheep, to be the victorious conquerors of the earth, to stand in boldness against the rulers of this world and to overcome it. How can such defenseless creatures ever even stand a chance? The answer is that we can't. Our only chance at victory is to follow the One who has already defeated this world. "If the LORD is my shepherd," do I truly want to follow Him, or am I expecting Him to follow me? What does it mean to be truly shepherded by Him? That seems so scary and uncertain. It means I must give up my right to myself and allow Him to lead me where He thinks I should go. It means that this "you" must become His "ewe."

This Bible study may be different from any other one you have done, for the aim of this study is not to gain more knowledge and understanding as much as it is about letting go of knowledge and understanding that you already have. This will be our first and greatest lesson in Becoming Ewe, we don't have to "know," we simply have to learn to follow the One who does. Even as I write this now, I am still grappling with implementing this lesson in my own life. After studying Psalm 23, reading every book on sheep and shepherding that I could get my hands on for the past few months, and praying and planning for this Bible study, I must admit that when I sat down to write this out I still felt unprepared. That little voice in my head that I try not to listen to began whispering to me, "Rhonda, you have never even spent time with any real sheep outside of the ones in a petting zoo." Frantically, I began racing through the address book in my mind, "Who do I know who might have some connection to sheep?" I thought about my friends who have kids in FFA, as well as my friends who live in or near the country. Sadly, I even thought of going back to the petting zoo. I prayed, "Lord, please let me at least touch a sheep before I begin writing this, or even better, if You could let me hold a lamb I know I would be so much more prepared." It did not take long for the tears to fill my eyes as He reminded me once again of how often I have "Touched The Lamb." Even sweeter, He reminded me of how often the Lamb has held me. "Rhonda, you are ready. Once again, I am leading you and guiding you through this," my sweet Shepherd reminded me. So, it is my greatest prayer that you too will know what it is to "touch the Lamb" through this study. And to know what it is to experience the weightless beauty that comes when we are able to shed every burden and take up our one true calling in this world: to know, love, and follow our Shepherd. I am so honored, humbled, and blessed to walk through this journey with you.

Welcome, precious lamb, to Becoming Ewe.

WEEK 1 BECOMING EWE

Day 1

A Lamb's Look at the Lamb

DAILY GRAIN	Please begin by prayerfully receiving God's Word to you through this Scripture. *Come, I will show you the Bride, the wife of the Lamb (Revelation 21:9b)*

Throughout the Bible, there is a theme. It runs from the very beginning at creation to the very end at the Revelation. This theme is what makes the Bible the most beautiful love story ever told. We have all heard that the Bible is God's love story to us, but few of us have lived that and know what it is to be loved and in love with the Great Shepherd. What do we think of when we imagine God as our Shepherd, and what does this have to do with love?

Take a moment here to record your thoughts about how you perceive God as a shepherd.

In what ways does His role as your Shepherd portray His love for you?

I was at a wedding recently when our table conversation turned towards answering the question, "What was the best wedding you ever attended?" As I listened to the answers of each person, I began to notice a certain theme. There was one story in particular that really touched my heart and truly embodied the theme that was coming to life through each of our stories. It was about a young woman who had grown up in church, but had fallen in love with a man who did not know God. She became pregnant, and because of that, the couple decided to marry. During the marriage, the man became abusive to this young lady. Not only that, she soon discovered that he had lied to her about many things. Even so, she wanted to stay in the marriage because of her vows, as well as to provide a father for the baby that was on the way. Before her son was even born, she was devastated to find that her husband had left her and taken all of their savings with him. Penniless and broken, she had no choice but to move back in with her parents. Not only had she been devastated by the failure of her marriage and by the fact that she was now going to be raising a son all by herself, but perhaps, even worse, she felt an overwhelming sense of shame as every choice she had made seemed to be coming back and taunting her, "You deserve this after disobeying God." She dreaded returning to church most of all, the church that she had all but forgotten as she had set out to make the most of her relationship with her husband. Yet, where else could she go? She knew that she needed Jesus more than ever now. The friends who she had not called or visited during her time in the marriage, the friends who she was sure would reject her now, embraced her and wrapped their arms around her, so happy to welcome her home into their hearts once more. They assured her that they would be with her as she brought this baby boy into the world. She felt loved and comforted by them, and all of the sudden, the fear and shame that had been overwhelming her began to somehow seem smaller and less intimidating. She continued attending church after giving birth to her son. As she was learning to trust Jesus as she never had before, God brought a new minister to their church, a young man who had been praying for a wife. This new mom seemed to be the least likely choice. However, the minute he met her, he loved her and knew that she was the wife he had been praying for. Her fear and shame caused her to resist him for some time, but eventually she began to allow herself the grace to believe that God might just be offering her the chance to redeem her broken past through the gift of this man.

There was not a dry eye in the church the morning they wed. This man who, in purity, had waited for Jesus to reveal to him his bride, stood waiting for this woman who had been devastated by impurity to walk towards him and become his wife. Many had been to weddings where the bride and groom's purity had made them all the more beautiful, but this wedding was different. The story of redemption made this wedding even more beautiful. Redemption always outshines perfection. At the altar, a huge cross had been erected, draped in white. The bride had requested this. She wanted everyone to know and understand that it was only through the cross that this day was made possible. And as she watched her son carry the rings down the aisle toward her soon-to-be husband, her heart burst with the awareness of Christ's ability to make any ashes we bring to Him into a crown of beauty. With tear stained cheeks, her father walked her down the aisle, not to the wedding march, but to the words of a song that this young woman had come to receive life from: "Lead me to the cross, where Your love poured out. Bring me to my knees, Lord; I lay me down. Rid me of myself. I belong to You. Lead me, lead me the cross."

Redemption! It is the theme we see all through God's love story for us, His Bible. And redemption has everything to do with the Lamb.

> In your own words, what does redemption mean to you?

> In what ways have you seen, or are now seeing God work the miracle of redemption in your own life?

Before we get into Psalm 23, the Shepherd's Psalm, we will spend this week reflecting on the heart of our Shepherd. And perhaps, more precious, we will allow our Shepherd the opportunity to reflect on our hearts. "For the LORD sees not as man sees: man looks on the outward appearance, but the LORD looks on the hearts." (1 Samuel 16:7b).

Sometimes it seems easier to strive to look at God's heart, but He came so that He could look on ours. Without His examination of our own hearts, we get nowhere with God.

> Is there any part of your heart that you feel apprehensive about having Him looking upon right now?

"There is therefore now no condemnation for those who are in Christ Jesus. For the law of the Spirit of life has set you free in Christ Jesus from the law of sin and death," (Romans 8:1-2). We are such sheep! We are unwilling to rob a bank, or disobey traffic laws, yet we so often fail to acknowledge the liberty that Jesus died for us to have the right to live by. He destroyed the law of sin and death so that we no longer have to obey that law. We are free in Him to obey the Spirit of Life. When we tolerate sin or shame in our lives, we are actually breaking God's law. So often we even sentence ourselves to self-appointed jails, where we stay until we either die or allow ourselves to let God's grace set us free.

Our first destination on this journey with our Shepherd begins with the words of the angel we see in Revelation 21:9b, "Come, I will show you the Bride, the wife of the Lamb." That Bride is you, beloved. Allow yourself to contemplate this image with me for a moment. You are standing at the beginning of a long aisle. You don't know or even understand how it happened, but you are dressed in a beautiful white gown, a wedding gown. Your feet go forward, almost without a thought. They are obeying a voice that comes from up ahead. Afraid, yet compelled, you look up and are overcome with emotion as you behold your Groom waiting for you at the end of the aisle. Power and majesty shine forth from Him, yet there is a gentle vulnerability in His eyes, like the eyes of a Lamb. As you dare to lock your eyes with His, you can't help but become enveloped in His love…and as you continue forward, you hear a song ringing out in the distance, "Lead me to the Cross, where Your love poured out. Bring me to my knees, Lord I lay me down. Rid me of myself. I belong to You…Lead me to the cross."

You are the Bride, Beloved, and this is your story of redemption. Welcome to Becoming Ewe. May you embrace the journey from you to ewe. Our destination is the place where the two become one, where the Bride and the Lamb collide at the cross.

Day 2

A Lamb's Look at the Lamb

	Please begin by prayerfully receiving God's Word to you through these Scriptures.
DAILY GRAIN	*Therefore a man shall leave his father and mother and hold fast to his wife, and they shall become one flesh. (Genesis 2:24)* *I am the good shepherd. The good shepherd lays down His life for the sheep. (John 10:11)* *Come, I will show you the Bride, the wife of the Lamb. (Revelation 21:9b)*

We left off yesterday with a wedding, perhaps God's most beautiful creation, where two people actually become one. Society's portrayal of marriage today can often skew the beauty of what God's perfect creation was intended to look like.

Meet me in Genesis 2:18-24 and let's catch a glimpse of the very first wedding ever performed here on earth.

Initial here once you have read it_____

Talk about a wedding march! The first wedding march, perhaps, sounded more like the hoofs and paws of animals as they marched past Adam, two by two, male and female, to receive their names, God's way of highlighting Adam's need for a helper "fit for him." Almost as soon as Adam began to experience and identify with his need, God already began to provide.

Verse 21 shows how the very first bride came to be. Answer the questions below about verse 21.

Who was responsible for "procuring" this First Bride? God or Adam?

Is there a need you have in your life right now? Is God "highlighting" an awareness in your life about a specific need? If so, share what it is below.

Who is responsible for "procuring" your need? God or you?

God is the supplier of each of our needs. Many of us waste so much time in our lives striving to meet perceived needs when God not only is the only One who truly knows what we need, but also is the only One who can provide. Sometimes He waits for us to move out of the role of "shepherding our own lives" before He provides. He is a God of order and we must move into alignment with Him before we can experience our Shepherd's provision for us.

I love that not only was Adam asleep when His greatest need for fulfillment was being brought to fruition, but that God used part of Adam to provide what he was lacking. God goes out of His way to show that we, like Adam, have nothing to offer God in helping fulfill our needs. He is our LORD and our Shepherd and knows how to provide best for us, even when we are unaware of His work. In fact, Adam's only contribution to meeting his need was his rib. Lying inside of him all along was the root answer to the deepest longing of his heart.

How like God to show us that He has placed inside of us all along all that we can or ever should need.

2nd Peter 1:3 speaks to this, "His divine power has granted to us all things that pertain to life and godliness, through the knowledge of him, who called us to his own glory and excellence."

Inside of each of us lies a longing, a desire for God that only He can fill. When we turn to Him with a heart that is ready to admit our own lack and need for Him, He fills us with Himself. The rib was already inside of Adam, yet had not been transformed into the object of his fulfillment. Similarly, God has planted in each of us the desire for Christ's life in us, which upon our awareness and belief in Him becomes our greatest source of fulfillment.

I find it both intriguing and beautiful that the very first marriage involved blood, pain, and the hand of God. It was a surgery of sorts; one became two, so that those two can ultimately become one. According to marriage tradition, the bride's walk down the aisle on her wedding day is symbolic of a blood covenant. As the bride and groom's family is each seated on separate sides of the aisle, the bride's walk down the aisle portrays the cutting through the blood to make one new family. Not long ago the church aisles were often lined in red to portray this tradition all the more. The day I married my husband I was blissfully unaware of how much God's first wedding would resemble my own. Blood and pain were the last things on my mind as I "cut covenant" with my man and became his bride. However, ten years later I can't say that our lives together much resemble the bliss of our wedding day. There has surely been pain, and I dare say, even some blood. Yet, above all else, there has been the miracle of God's hand allowing us two to become one. Too often, like Adam, I have been asleep to the greater miracle of marriage that has been taking place in our lives. Marriage is what has happened while I have all too often been wrapped up in lesser things. Marriage is what God has used, more than any other creation of His, to sharpen me, and mold me and to make me more like Himself. I find such truth in Adam's words, "This at last is bone of my bones and flesh of my flesh; she shall be called Woman because she is taken out of Man." In our journey here upon the pastures of God's grace, He causes us, His Bride, to journey through the blood, pain, and His own hand to become one with Him. Not all of us here will have a husband with skin on. However, all of us who know Jesus will know what it is to be a bride. Let's spend some time looking into a few verses that will bring to life what I am talking about.

Meet me in John 19:28-35 please answer the questions below.

In verse 28, how does Jesus describe what he is experiencing?

> How does this relate with what Adam may have experienced as God pointed out to him that each animal had a helper, but he did not?

> In verse 30, what happens to Jesus?

How does this relate to what happened to Adam as his bride was made?

In verse 35, where is Jesus pierced? What comes out of His side?

How does this relate to Adam and what came out of his side?

"I am the good shepherd. The good shepherd lays down His life for the sheep." John 10:11

"For no one ever hated his own flesh, but nourishes and cherishes it, just as Christ does the Church, because we are members of His body. Therefore a man shall leave his father and mother and hold fast to his wife, and the two shall become one flesh. This mystery is profound, and I am saying that it refers to Christ and the Church. Ephesians 5:29-32

"Come and I will show you the Bride, the wife of the Lamb" Revelation 21:9b

Beloved, do you now see? You are the bride, taken out the side of your groom, while He was asleep. Right there, at the cross, pain, death, blood, and the Hand of God collided to fulfill a covenant that He made with you before you were born. God reached down from heaven and provided a surgery on Adam's sin-struck descendants and pulled a bride right out of the side of Jesus. He reached into the Lamb, and made two where there had only been one. Before that moment, there was no way for a sinful man to become one with our righteous God. At that moment, Jesus made a way for us to become one with Himself.

Too often, at the very heart of our unwillingness to follow God and let Him shepherd our lives, lies resentment. We resent that He wants to lead us without knowing us. Rules without relationship always lead to resentment. Too often we see God not as He truly is, but as a Divine set of rules we must follow. We know He went to the cross and died for our sins, but our hearts long for more of His life, not merely His death. We don't always identify with the fact that He willingly became a lamb long before He asked to be our Shepherd. He lived a life identifying with our pain and rejection (Isaiah 53). In ways that we can't see or imagine, His experience in becoming one with us was so much more than any trials we will face here on earth. There has only ever been one Jesus who walked on this earth, one man who was also God. Talk about being misunderstood! We think of His death, but we seldom think of His life. He lived here 33 years with not one person that He could fully relate to. And yet, even though He was God. He set aside His glory to become a servant, a lamb who perfectly followed His Father's will.

In fact, let's take a look at Scripture that may better demonstrate what I am talking about.

"In the days of his flesh, Jesus offered up prayers and supplications, with loud cries and tears to him who was able to save him from death, and he was heard because of his reverence. Although he was a son, he learned obedience through what he suffered." Hebrews 5:7-8

How does this Scripture identify what Jesus' walk here on earth was like?

Based on the above verse, who was shepherding Jesus during His life here on earth?

Long before we were born, He came to show us how to walk out our journey here on earth. He became the Lamb not only so that He could die for us, but also to show us how to live for Him. You are and always have been perfectly loved.

If you ever want to know how much you are loved, take a listen to His prayer for you in John 17. Listen to how His heart longs for you to know Him and to understand Him. How He longs for you to be with Him and to know the oneness that can only come through His love. He gave His whole life entrusting Himself to you, reaching out to you with every breath. And in His death, he paid for you. He does ask to be Shepherd of your life, but He asks in love. Not as one who wants the right to rule over you, but as one who wants to love you and lead you to places that are far greater and with more eternal impact than you can imagine. He asks for you to become His Bride, one who is willing to lay aside her own right to rule because she loves and trusts the Shepherd more than she loves her life.

"Therefore a man shall leave his father and mother and hold fast to his wife, and they shall become one flesh." Genesis 2:24. Do you see Beloved? He already left everything to come and know and be known by you? There is no need for resentment or fear. He doesn't even ask for you to feel love for Him before you choose to follow Him. "We love because He first loved us," 1 John 4:19. He is asking, "Will you let me let Me love you? Will you marry Me?"

And if we are willing, Beloved, you and I get to spend the rest of our lives walking down His aisle of grace until the two at last become fully one and You become fully Ewe, the Lamb and His Bride. How I pray that this might just be the day that He leads you to a mirror and says to you, "Come and I will show you the Bride, the wife of the Lamb."

Please close in prayer thanking Jesus for making you His Bride.

Day 3

A Lambs Look At The Lamb

DAILY GRAIN	Please begin by prayerfully receiving God's Word to you through these Scripture(s): *"And the rib that the LORD God had taken from the man he made into a woman and brought her to the man." Genesis 2:22* *"Therefore a man shall leave his father and mother and hold fast to his wife, and they shall become one flesh." Genesis 2:24* *"Then the eyes of both were opened, and they knew that they were naked. And they sewed fig leaves together and made themselves loincloths." Genesis 3:7*

About now, you may be thinking to yourself, "I thought this was a Bible study about sheep?" If you are, you are partly right. There are many aspects of a sheep's life that will come into play later on in our study. However, more than sheep, this study is about allowing yourself to *become* someone new. Knowledge about God and even about ourselves, without love gets us nowhere. If this study is about one thing, it is about finally getting to where you were always meant to be with God. We have spent so much time discussing weddings this week because it is important to know that Jesus became a lamb before He ever asked us to become one.

In day one, we examined how, just as Woman was taken from the side of Adam, so we, His Bride, are taken from the side of Christ. Genesis 2:22 states, "And the rib that the Lord God had taken from the man he made into a woman and brought her to the man." The word for "made" in Hebrew gives a much richer definition. It defines it as "fashioned."

> In your own words, descried the difference between the words *made* and *fashioned*?

I love to picture God *fashioning* the first woman. There is such intention implied with that word. I also love that she was fashioned from a rib. As I ponder God's choice material to begin His creation with, I can't help but compare it to His choice material from which He created Adam.

> In Genesis 2:7, we catch a glimpse of God at work in forming Adam. What is Adam formed from?

> Why do you think God chose dust from which to form Adam?

> What made Adam "a living creature?"

I find it interesting that we see here in Scripture a mention of God breathing into Adam, with the result being that Adam becomes a living creature. We don't see this in His fashioning of woman. Instead, we get a picture of God taking living rib from Adam's side and making her into a helper that is "*fit for him.*"

Why do you think God created a woman out of Adam's rib?

Scripture does not tell us everything, but I know from human anatomy that the rib is a bone that is used to not only give posture to a human body, but perhaps its greatest purpose is in guarding the heart and lungs. The heart represents the mechanism that allows the life of a human (the blood) to move through the body, while the lungs give a human being breath. All and all, I see God's purpose in creating women from a rib as His way of showing her what her purpose is. Just as man was created from dirt and for dirt (to have dominion over the land), so woman was created from man's rib because she is to be his helper, the guardian of his heart and breath. She is also to be at his side, with him through life. The hole left in his side in her formation leaves vulnerability in him that only she fills.

And just as we have seen this week, the first marriage sets a pattern for a greater marriage, which was to come; the marriage between Christ and us, His church.

While it may be hard to acknowledge our role as the guardian of our husband's heart and breath (that is a whole other Bible study), it is not hard to acknowledge that this is our role as Christ's Bride, the church.

Look up the following verses and record what they say about Jesus' purpose for the church.

Matthew 28:18-20

Mark 16:15-18

Luke 24:44-49

If you ask me, He gave us quite the responsibility when He entrusted us with His breath (the Word) and His heart (His Presence).

So far we have talked about why God fashioned women from the rib. However, I would like to spend the rest of our time today contemplating on the word "fashion" itself.

As we look back at Genesis 2:25 we see that, "And the man and his wife were both naked and not ashamed." It is so strange to think about not wearing clothes, and perhaps even stranger to think about not being ashamed about it. However, how beautiful to live in such a perfect world that clothes are not necessary.

Please list below at least three purposes that clothes serve.

Read Genesis 3:1-8 and then answer the questions below.

In verse 7, what is the very first thing that happened after they ate?

In find it ironic that their first response to having their "eyes opened" was to want to cover themselves. I don't know about you, but I am taken back when I try to imagine what it must mean to have your "eyes opened." We know that Adam and his wife were both perfect, and therefore there was no disease to mar their eye sight. Based on Hebrews 11:1, "Faith is the assurance of things hoped for, the conviction of things not seen." I assume that having their "eyes opened" pertained to sin coming into their hearts and, for the first time in their lives, they are experiencing distance from and doubt in God. They had once walked in perfect faith in God, never once thinking to question whether or not He was holding out on them. The minute sin enters, they become suddenly aware of the insecurity that it brings with it and their first response is to cover up.

Verse 7 contains the Bible's very first mention of clothes, what were the first clothes made from?

Verse 8 mentions that they were hiding among the trees. In God's Word, what we are dressed in has symbolic meaning for where our hearts are. In other words, what we place on our body tells so much about what is in our hearts. In this verse, we can see that Adam and his wife have covered themselves up with the same material in which they are hiding from God in.

> As we look back at Genesis 3:7, what type of leaves did Adam and his wife cover themselves with?

I find this very interesting. If we look ahead to Matthew 21:18-21, we will see another encounter with a fig tree. Let's read those verses and answer the questions below.

> How does verse 18 describe Jesus?

> In verse 19, what does Jesus find on the tree?

> How does he respond?

This is so cool, I still get chills as I contemplate it. In the Bible, fig leaves are symbolic of false religion. Jesus is hungry. His physical need points us all to a greater truth. Any other source we seek for filling will prove to leave us hungry. When we are hungry, there is only one fruit that satisfies and it is found on our Tree of Life: Jesus. How I pray that you and I will stay, "filled with the fruit of righteousness that comes through Jesus Christ, to the glory and praise of God." Philippians 1:11.

As we look back at Adam and his wife cowering in the fig leaves that they are hiding in, I can honestly say that the apple does not fall far from the tree. We are still up to the same old tricks. Just as our first parents dressed themselves up in the same material that they were hiding from God in, so many of us do the same. We present the world with a picture of who and what we want to be. We don't even know better, and we surely would not call what we are doing "false religion"; however we will soon find out that what we wear on the outside has everything to do with what is wrong on the inside of us. How it must have broken the heart of God to see His children dressed in clothes to cover up the way He made them. The truth about the glory He had placed in them, "naked and not ashamed," was now covered over. The very essence of true purity and innocence was now covered over with man's attempt to hide in self made material. I catch tiny glimpses of what He must have felt as I watch my daughters begin to strive to become someone who others want to them to be instead of taking delight in who God made them. I never want them to "wear" something out of insecurity. I want them to dress themselves up in what complements all the ways that God has made them beautiful. It wasn't the leaves on them that broke God's heart, it was what the leaves represented; their hearts being separate from His. One of the most beautiful truths I have learned about the differences between God's love and false religion is that God is always about taking off, not adding to. He allows us to strip away what confines and restrains, where man-made religion is always binding us, adding more and more upon us until we feel crushed under its demands. I believe this is the reason why so many have turned away from church and are afraid to encounter Christ. "A little yeast leavens the whole lump." Galatians 5:9. And a few fig leaves can lead many to missing the freedom to be naked and unafraid in God's presence.

In what ways might you have experienced the dryness that comes with the "fig leaves" in your life?

We each have our own set of "fig leaves" that we dress up in during times of insecurity. If you can recognize what yours are, please share them below. You don't have to share them with your group, but sometimes just the simple act of writing them down symbolizes the first step towards taking them off.

It seems ironic, but for me my "fig leaves" often involve ministry. Sometimes when God really wants to do a work in me, I will run and try and "cover" myself in good works. This is one of the most deceptive forms of "fig leaves" for it gives us the illusion of being close to God. As you will discover through our study, I have a long history of insecurity. It is still sometimes hard for me to truly believe that God cares more about my heart than what I can produce with my hands. I have trouble believing Him when He has said, "My grace is sufficient for you, for my power is made perfect in weakness." (2 Corinthians 12:9). It is still hard for me to see my weaknesses and to not want to cover them up. Only in Him are we able to rejoice as we lay them at the foot of the cross and watch Him turn our mess into a beautiful message.

One reason that I love the analogy of our walk here on Earth as lambs is the fact that lambs must be shorn in order to thrive. In God's wisdom, He knew that we, like lambs, need to be shorn too from the weight of this world in order to survive.

In fact, let's close today laying our wool (and fig leaves) at His feet as we pray and ask Him to bring us out of hiding. In the space below there is a lamb, let's take some time shearing the wool off of it by writing down what may be weighing on us in our lives right now. We may feel naked underneath it all, but we are also sure to feel lighter.

Day 4

A Lambs Look At The Lamb

DAILY GRAIN	Please begin by prayerfully receiving God's Word to you through these Scripture(s): *"The man called his wife's name Eve, because she was the mother of all living. And the LORD God made for Adam and for his wife garments of skins and clothed them." Genesis 3:20-21* *"The night is far gone; the day is at hand. So then let us cast off the works of darkness and put on the armor of light. Let us walk properly as in the daytime, not in orgies and drunkenness, not in sexual immorality and sensuality, not in quarreling and jealousy. But put on the Lord Jesus Christ, and make no provision for the flesh." Romans 13:12-14*

So far this week we have focused on what Adam and his wife dressed themselves in after the Fall. Today we will shift focus onto what God dressed them in. Read the verse below and answer the questions that follow.

"The man called his wife's name Eve, because she was the mother of all living. And the LORD God made for Adam and for his wife garments of skins and clothed them." Genesis 3:20-21

What is one thing you notice about the woman in this verse?

Yes, she gets a name. We have been talking this week about the theme of redemption that runs throughout the Bible. In your own opinion, how does her name, Eve, point to redemption?

Beloved, don't you just love it? In ancient times, names not only signified what one was called, but also his or her purpose and reason for being. I love that Eve did not get her name until after the Fall. Speaking of her name, is anyone but me a little curious about how Adam ascertained that she was to be "the mother of all living" just after God had presented the curse?

Let's go back a little and find out more about how he came to this conclusion. Meet me in Genesis 3:14-16. Let's read these verses and then answer the questions below.

Who does God curse in verses 14-15? What does this have to do with the woman?

I think it is so cool that woman's ability to help God in creating life, is first mentioned in the serpent's curse. He thought that he had just done in God's favorite creation and here he finds out that there are going to be many, many more. His worst nightmare has just come true. Out of death we see the hope of Life springing forth, the hope of Jesus redeeming us back to God.

Fill in the blanks based on verse 15

_____ shall bruise your _____,

and _____ shall bruise his _____.

I don't know about you, but a bruise to the heel seems slight compared to the bruise to the head, which is often fatal.

As we skip down to verse 16 we find Eve's consequence being handed down. Once again, we see the allusion to life springing up in the midst of pain. I don't know about you, but as a wife and mother, without Christ, these two consequences of sin are about enough to do me in. Did I mention that I am in the midst of parenting a teenage girl? Surely God's consequence of "in pain you shall bring forth children" extends through raising them. It has been the most rewarding and challenging job of my life. However, as challenging as that and everything else that is thrown at me in this life can become, Jesus always overrules. "My desire shall be for my husband (Christ) and he shall rule over me." (based on Gen. 3:16b). As long as I keep Him first, no pain I face is insurmountable.

I laugh as I try and picture the scene just after these consequences of sin are announced. He has just received his devastating consequences, and yet his first response is to turn towards his wife and name her Eve; the mother of all living.

It tickles me because I have a child that his response reminds me of. Her ever-optimistic outlook can see the silver lining in the worst of consequences. Once we had to miss a trip to the pool because she refused to clean her room in time. Her response was, "I am kind of happy because that water really burns my eyes." As Adam listened to the words of God, I'm sure that he was looking for that one word, the word that had scared him into staying away from the tree during the time before the Fall.

> Let's take a look back in Genesis 2:15-17. Write below what God said would happen if Adam ate from the tree of knowledge of good and evil?

As we look back through Adam's consequence for sin, we don't see the word death, but we see, "By the sweat of your face you shall eat bread, till you return to the ground, for out of it you were taken, for you are dust, and to dust you shall return." Gen. 3:19.

> Let's take a look back at Genesis 2:7 where we find the creation of man. What was man made from?

What action on the part of God made him a living creature?

The breath of God is what made Adam come to life. We see that he does not physically die at the Fall, which leads us to believe that death as we know it is not what God had been referring to in Genesis 2:15-17.

We see God's story of redemption right here in the very beginning. We chose death, we chose to be separate from the very One who breathed us to life, yet He chooses to redeem our life back for us.

He gave a man of dust life from His own breath, and man handed it back to Him. Yet, He gives it back to us, He refuses to let us give up on life. As Psalm 103:14 explains, "For he knows our frame, he remembers that we are dust."

In the midst of what should be a death sentence, He extends the hope of life. Like Adam who displays the very first of words of faith, "she was the mother of all living," so we must learn in this world, that is so tainted by sin, to look past the pain of it all and respond to the offer of life that is being displayed through God's Word.

Genesis 3:21 displays the ramifications of Adam and Eve's actions. In this verse, we see the first death on Earth.

Who was the killer?

To whom did the first death happen?

The Word does not say what type of animal it was that was slain in order to cover over Adam and Eve's nakedness. However, I picture it being the skin of a Lamb, a precious reminder of the greater sacrifice that was one day to come and cover over our sins once and for all.

An all-powerful God must reach down and slay His own beloved creation, one of whom He had said, "It is good." (Genesis 1:25.) Adam could only stand powerlessly and watch as one of his beloved companions, one who had been his only comfort before Eve was made, was slain to cover his sin.

There was death, blood, and the Hand of God reaching down to show man his need for reconciliation with God. The blood poured out, washing over Adam and Eve's sinful choice, and providing a skin for them: a garment fashioned for them by God Himself.

Further on in history, we see a new story. God will no longer take off the skin, but will put it on.

"When Christ came into the world, he said, 'Sacrifices and offerings you have not desired, but a body you have prepared for me; in burnt offerings and sin offerings, you have taken no pleasure.'" Hebrews 10:5-6

Two, God and man, became one, offering us the chance to become one with God.

While driving a few weeks ago, I realized that my inspection sticker had expired. As soon as I became aware of my violation, paranoia swept over me. I was on the lookout for cops every time I drove my car. Anxiety swept through my body each time I saw one. I had many opportunities to go in and get the new sticker, but it never seemed like the right time. One day as I was taking my daughter to school, there was police car parked right in the middle lane, I was sure that he was going to see my violation and catch me. He didn't. But, as I dropped my daughter off I realized that I was letting my irresponsibility in not taking care of my violation keep me from the freedom in driving my car. I took time out that day to make it a priority to get my inspection sticker. The next day I must have driven by at least four police cars and never once felt that anxiety.

Jesus came to offer us a way through which we can remove any violation we have within ourselves. As long as the violation is there, we stay in hiding and bound to the very thing that Christ came to set us free from. Too often, we don't take responsibility for our violation before God, and therefore we can't experience the freedom He wants us to have. He has already taken complete responsibility for His part in reaching down to fashion us in the covering of His Son. We must do our part in reaching up to receive all that He is offering to us.

"The night is far gone; the day is at hand. So then let us cast off the works of darkness and put on the armor of light. Let us walk properly as in the daytime, not in orgies and drunkenness, not in sexual immorality and sensuality, not in quarreling and jealousy. But put on the Lord Jesus Christ, and make no provision for the flesh." Romans 13:12-14

Let's close today by taking responsibility for any violation that might be holding us back from living in the perfect peace that Christ's blood affords us.

Day 5

A Lambs Look At The Lamb

<table>
<tr>
<td>DAILY GRAIN </td>
<td>Please begin by prayerfully receiving God's Word to you through these Scriptures:

"He drove out the man, and at the east of the garden of Eden he placed the cherubim and a flaming sword that turned every way to guard the way to the tree of life." Genesis 3:24

"What man of you, having a hundred sheep, if he has lost one of them, does not leave the ninety-nine in the open country, and go after the one that is lost, until he finds it? And when he has found it, he lays it on his shoulders, rejoicing." Luke 15:4-5</td>
</tr>
</table>

We have spent this week looking at the very first time that two became one, God's perfect man and woman entering in to the first marriage. This week we have discovered the theme of redemption that began with the Fall, and continues all throughout God's Word, extending into each of our hearts. The miracle of God's grace, which caused the two to become one, allows you and I to become perfectly one with our God and Savior.

We will leave the garden today, but not before gleaning one last look at how the theme of redemption plays out in the story.

Let's jump right in. Meet me in Genesis 3:22-24. Read the verse and then answer the questions that follow.

In verse 22, what reason does God give for causing Adam and Eve to leave the garden?

What does verse 22 say would happen if Adam and Eve ate from the tree of Life?

What would be the tragedy in Adam and Eve eating and living forever in their current state?

Right from the very beginning, we see God acting in a way to begin His plan of redeeming His children. Had He given up on them, and given them over to death fully, He would not have hesitated in allowing them to eat from the Tree of Eternal Life, sealing them away from Him in sin forever.

Now, let's read verses 23-24 and answer the questions that follow.

Verse 24 mentions that, "He drove out the man." In what way might this act reflect God's shepherding of His children?

How did God protect the garden from being re-entered?

We saw the new roles being born as God brought woman to Adam. Similarly, here we see another role being born, that of God as our Shepherd. Before the Fall, Adam and his wife had no need for a Shepherd, as they were in perfect communion with God. There was not even the idea in their minds not to obey, trust, and love Him. However, as they allowed the forbidden fruit to enter his mouth, he was in essence saying, "I desire to become my own shepherd more than I desire you, God."

It is both ironic and comforting that the very thing Adam had wanted to elude in God's providence becomes the very vehicle that God uses to begin his redemption. Whether we like it or not, whether we think we need Him or not, the LORD is our Shepherd, we shall not want. Despite our actions, He never gives up on coming after His children.

> How does this truth impact you? Is there any aspect of your life right now that God may be trying to convince you that He is Shepherd over? If so, why not take the space below and write out a prayer of surrender to Him right now.

In verse 24, we see two words placed together that, as Christians, we hold so dear. Those words are "the way." It tenders my heart that those words, the very words that we see associated with what is lost at the Fall, being used to call the earliest Christians.

> Look up Acts 9:2 and write down the name of the group of people that Saul is wanting to bring back to Jerusalem.

It gives me chills as I see God's story of redemption being played out in real life. The way that had been blocked now opens for all who would believe in the One who has become our way. Let's take a look in John 14:1-7 as we see the fruition of our way being opened back for us through the Life of Christ.

> In John 14:1-3, what is Jesus describing?

> How does this relate to what Adam and Eve lost in the Fall?

In verses 4-7, we see Jesus describing Himself as "the Way, the Truth, and the Life." I love how in verse 4, He states, "and you know the way to where I am going." Often, I compare myself to Thomas. I know Jesus, but I don't know how to make my knowledge of Him play out in my "Ways" of walking through this life. He often reminds me of this passage and says, "Rhonda, I am your WAY." And each time, my heart is broken by my own lack of faith. Like a sheep, I want a path instead of a Shepherd. Still, He loves me too much to let me walk through this journey while missing out on the joy of what this life is truly all about: knowing and experiencing the love of our Shepherd.

Like me, have you often been tempted to exchange Him (your Way) for a path?

Too often, this plays itself out in my life with Christ. If I don't watch it, I can soon fall into the trap of allowing my walk with Him to become a "to-do" list as opposed to a way of being. This study is all about Becoming. We, who are so quick to want to check boxes off of a list, can easily fall prey to exchanging His Becoming for our tasks.

This was such a struggle for me that I actually wrote a poem about it a few years back. It is a poem written in the form of a prayer;

Romans 12 :1 & 2 "I appeal to you brothers, by the mercies of God, to present your bodies as a living sacrifice, holy and acceptable to God, which is your spiritual worship. Do not be conformed to this world, but BE transformed by the renewal of your mind, that by testing you may discern what is the will of God, what is good and acceptable and perfect."

Do vs. Be
There is a war in me
I'd like to think there's more to this
Than what I choose to see

Do vs. Be
When will I ever see
That life is more than what I do..
It's Whose I choose to be

Do Vs. Be
LORD, teach my eyes to see
That only through
Abiding in You

Can I hope to be …

More than what I bargained for
Your Love makes me who I am
And through You I can be more
Than this dust can understand

So I give You LORD my well-worn list
My do's and don'ts in exchange for Your "Be"
And in Your Hands I will discover more
Than these simple eyes could ever see

Forgive me LORD when I hem You in
With my plans of what I'll do
And thank You LORD that You don't let me find rest
Until I again abide in You

For You are my "Be," You are my rest
My only worth is found in You
And may this foolish self never again believe
That my worth is in my "do"

Beloved, like me, have you often struggled with finding your worth outside of Christ alone? Why not write out your own message of surrender right here. Make a point to trade in your to-do list in exchange for His "be."

John 14:7 really touches my heart and brings home what we are learning about right here, how Jesus paved the Way back into the garden of God's love for us. "If you had known me, you would have known the Father also. From now on, you do know Him and have seen Him."

It is often hard to think of our Way as being a relationship instead of a path. However, here on Earth, there is no other way to gain ground in Heaven than through knowing the One who is our Way. What a shame it would be to stand before Him one day and to realize that we spent our whole lives seeking a path when all He really wanted was a relationship with us.

When I first married my husband, I just knew I would become the best wife ever. I spent the first six years of our marriage reading every marriage book on the market, attending Bible studies on how to become the perfect married couple. All the while, I resented him for not putting forth the same effort to make our marriage better. I bought him book after book, invited him to conferences, and even, I am ashamed to say, resorted to threatening him with the "D" word if he did not shape up and start making our marriage a priority. One day, while in yet *another* Bible study about being a better wife, the LORD spoke very loudly to me. We had been studying over David and Jonathan, and we were in 1 Samuel 18 and as I read through verse 3-4, the LORD opened my eyes and broke my heart. The verse states, "Then Jonathan made a covenant with David, because he loved him as his own soul. And Jonathan stripped himself of the robe that was on him and gave it to David, and his armor and even his sword and his bow and his belt." As soon as I read the verses, I could hear in my spirit God telling me, "You don't love your husband as yourself." I almost shot up with an indignant reply, "What do you mean? I seem to be the only one who cares about our marriage." However, before I could utter a word, my eyes fell upon verse 4 and I could sense the LORD asking me, "After Jonathan stripped off his clothing and gave it to David, what do you suppose he was wearing?" "LORD, he must have put on David's stinky, shepherd clothes." Tears flooded my eyes as I hit the floor in repentance for my own lack of love and compassion towards my husband. God knew me and allowed me to teach a Bible study while I did not love the one who God had given me as my primary love in this life with the same love as I loved myself. I was like Jonathan, who God had made royalty and given the finest robes to wear. Each morning, even in my sin, God never failed to dress me up in His love and majesty. However, instead of using my robes to clothe those around me, especially my husband, I used them to parade around my home, in essence saying, "Look at *my* robes. Don't you wish you had robes like mine?" Like Jonathan, I had never once thought to take off what God had wrapped around me and, in turn, wrap them around the shoulders of my husband so that he might share in the love of Christ with me. I had never offered to share in the weight of the load that he was carrying and to wear his robes that stunk with the debris of this world. I did not love him as myself. After all my time in His Word, I did not know how to love as He did. I had taught about it in Sunday school, but never once reached down to get my own robe dirty in the mess of someone else's life. I did not really understand what it was to follow Jesus and to truly let Him use me to love as He loves, to lay down my life for another. I must say, that was the most humbled I have ever been. It took me two days of tears and repentance before I was ready to begin a new day, a day where I no longer wore His robes in order to display His glory, but I wore them in order to share His glory with anyone who would allow me, beginning with my husband.

Is there anyone in your life whom God might be asking you to love as you love yourself right now? If so, please share about what God is impressing upon your heart below.

As we finish up this week's lesson, I would like for us to take a look at our verses in Gen. 3:24, "He drove out the man, and at the east of the garden of Eden he placed the cherubim and a flaming sword that turned every way to guard the way to the tree of life."

I cannot get the image of that "flaming sword" out of my mind as I contemplate how it is symbolic of our own journey back to the garden of God's love. Let's look at the following verses to get a clearer picture of what I mean. Next to each verse, write what the verse says about "flames" or a "sword" or both.

Isaiah 43:2-

Matthew 10:34-

Hebrews 4:12

Hebrews 12:29

1 Corinthians 3:13

Revelation 19:15

Revelation 20:14

Beloved, as we see here, there is no way for us to avoid the fire and the sword. The sword represents the Word of God and the fire is God's judgement, poured out on Christ at the cross. We will either walk through the sword of His truth, the Word of God, and allow it to become our Way, our Truth, and our Life, or we will walk into the sword and live eternally in the fire of judgement. God provided a way for us, through His own body. He walked through the flaming sword, taking the cutting and tearing of our judgement upon His own body, leaving an aisle of blood for us to walk through and enter back into the garden, back to where our Tree of Life stands forever.

Ephesians 6:17 exhorts us to, "take up the helmet of salvation, and the sword of the Spirit, which is the Word of God." The sword of God's Word once kept us out, but now it brings us in. Beloved, we have been given a treasure right here in our hands, the very breath of God! Just as He bent over Adam in the beginning, and breathed His Life into him, "and the man became a living creature," so God has reached down to us and given us His own breath. His Word is not just a book, it has a heartbeat, it is alive and it is making you alive in it. John 1:14 says, "And the Word became flesh and dwelt among us.... " Oh Beloved, let your flesh become His Word and dwell among Him. Let nothing in this world stop you from becoming one with Him.

Video Week 1

Letting the Shepherd Love Us So He Can Lead Us

Fill in the blanks below with these words according to the lesson;
home, if, self-will, light, home, darkness

Romans 8:1 *"There is therefore now no condemnation for those who are in Christ Jesus"*

_____ the LORD is your Shepherd, you shall not want.

Sheep never have a _____, the Shepherd is their _____.

We believe _____ rather than _____.

_____ _____ is the total negation of God's love.

Notes_____

_____

_____

_____

_____

_____

_____

Day 1

The LORD is my Shepherd

DAILY GRAIN	Please begin by prayerfully receiving God's Word to you through these Scripture(s): *"The LORD is my shepherd; I shall not want." Psalm 23:1*

I remember all too well the day that these words took on new depth in my soul. It had been a long and confusing time for my family and I, one of those seasons where every aspect of our lives seemed to have huge, neon, blinking question mark hanging over it. I remember the conversation with God, "Lord, can you at least give me something to hold on to? I don't even know how to prepare for what is coming." I did not have the courage to tell Him how I was really feeling, how I had been angry and confused by His lack of direction and guidance. If He is my Shepherd, why was He not shepherding me? Was I doing something wrong? Was I not having enough faith? I could not figure out why my Shepherd had allowed me to wander off seemingly so far from Him.

Then His answer came. It is amazing how such a small voice can create such a huge difference in our life and perspective. "Rhonda, *if* the LORD is your Shepherd, you shall not want." What a difference that one, tiny word makes! This meant that, in His care, I was lacking nothing. Even my desire to know was a "want" that revealed my own lack of trust in my Shepherd. As I contemplated that verse, my mind began to go crazy thinking of all that I had been striving for. Like a bouquet of balloons suddenly released in to the air, I began to see my list of "wants" drift from my heart in to the hands of my Shepherd.

What about you? What are you "wanting" right now? It may be something tangible or, like me, answers that only God can supply.

Take a moment here and pray for God to take these wants from your heart and mind in to His own hands. Initial here when you have finished_____.

Colossians 2:9-10 (ESV) says, "For in Him the whole fullness of the deity dwells bodily and you have been filled in Him, who is the head and rule of all authority." I love how The Message expresses this same verse, "Everything of God gets expressed in him, so you can see and hear him clearly. You don't need a telescope, a microscope, or a horoscope to realize the fullness of Christ, and the emptiness of the universe without him. When you come to him, that fullness comes together for you, too. His power extends over everything." In Christ, we truly have the freedom not to want. So much of what we are programmed for, even from our earliest moments, revolve around "wanting" or "not wanting." We want the good stuff and we want someone to get it for us. We don't want the bad stuff and we desperately want someone to save us from it. So often we have perceived God as being this type of provider for us. His job description for our lives, once we let Him in, pretty much entails keeping us away from "the bad stuff'" and giving us "the good stuff." Sadly, many of us perceive Him as a glorified version of Santa Claus instead of God of the universe, the Creator of everything, and our Savior.

> Take a moment right now to write down your true perceptions of God. Who is He to you right now?

> Are there ways He might be trying to break out of *who you think He is* to show you the truth about *who He really* is? If so, what in ways is He doing this?

If "the LORD is my shepherd," do I truly want to follow Him or am I expecting Him to follow me? What does it mean to truly be shepherded by Him? That seems so scary and uncertain. It means I must give up my right to myself and allow Him to lead me where He thinks I should go. "Lord, help me want to give myself to You. Help me stop wanting to be the shepherd of my life. I want to know You more and to be able to trust You with my journey here on Earth, but I don't always know how. Please accept this prayer as my cry for help. Come and get Your lamb and carry me across Your shoulders into Your will for my life, Jesus. I love You and I surrender to You, my faithful Shepherd. Amen."

> Did you find it challenging to pray the prayer above? If so, why? What are you experiencing right now? If you did not, what do you think is prohibiting you from praying it? Please share below.

"I shall not want." Can I even imagine what a life without wanting is? Is it even possible to "not want?" How do I get from here to there? I want to want You most and I know that I should, but there are so many voices in my head and heart that cry out for things in this world so much louder than they cry for You. "Lord, please help quiet the voices that cry out for anything other than You. Please teach me what it is to not want. Help me to crave You with such passion and longing that nothing else on Earth will ever compete. Begin showing me now what it is to follow You into heavenly places, to be so full in You that there is room for nothing more. Then overflow Your love and Presence in me so that those who encounter me will also encounter You. Amen."

> Did you find it challenging to pray the prayer above? If so, why? What are you experiencing right now? If you did not, what do you think is prohibiting you from praying it? Please share below.

Sweet One, you are on your way to the freedom that comes with truly living a life without wanting. "For in Christ all the fullness of Deity lives in bodily form, and you have been given fullness in Christ, who is the head over every power and authority," (Col. 2:9 NIV). How could we possibly desire more once our souls have been filled to the top with Jesus?

Day 2

The LORD is my Shepherd
"He makes me lie down in green pastures"

DAILY GRAIN	Please begin by prayerfully receiving God's Word to you through these Scriptures: *"He makes me lie down in green pastures." Psalm 23:2* *"Know that the LORD is God. It is he who made us; and we are his; we are his people, the sheep of his pasture." Psalm 100:3*

Right now, this very moment, I am in the midst of a miracle. I am a wife and mother of three very active children, all of which just happen to be gone for the entire weekend. I thought that I might go in shock once the silence set in (in a good way), but here I am and to be honest, I am a little scared. My inexperience with true silence has left me unprepared for the loudness of being alone. I cannot even remember what it is to be alone. However, as I meditate on the verses above, I am suddenly drenched in a new awareness that this precious silence is ushering me into the greater realization that I am really not, nor ever will be, alone. I am safe with my Shepherd. Even when everyone else is out of my sight, He never takes His eyes off of me. I "know that the LORD is God." It is He who made me, and I am His. I am His girl, and the ewe of His pasture. If I will let Him, God's presence will invade the silence in my life. Often the loudness of my fear is greater than the silence of my rest in Him.

What fears tend to become louder to you than God's voice?

Are there ways that you are able to quiet the fears in order to experience the silence of God's rest? If so, what are they?

"He makes me lie down in green pastures." What does that really mean? David, who spent the early part of his adult life as a shepherd, wrote this Psalm. His time spent shepherding prepared him for a greater role that was to come in his life: shepherding God's people, Israel. Like us, it did not take David long to realize his need for his own Shepherd. Also like us, it was out in the fields of his common day life that he learned to recognize and respond to the Great Shepherd. David knew from his time with the sheep that it is nearly impossible for them to lie down unless certain requirements are met: freedom from all fear, freedom from the friction with others of their kind, freedom from hunger, and freedom from the pests, parasites, and flies. Sound familiar girls? As a busy wife and mom, I am often discouraged at my own inability to stay in the peace that God's green pastures represent. It seems like I am always only one unexpected bill opening or one outbreak of sibling rivalry away from it. I feel very sheep-like as I ponder my own "laying down requirements." They seem so often to be based on circumstances, yet the peace that our Shepherd provides is not based on our circumstances but based on His presence. How often do we allow ourselves to truly rest in Him and forget all of our worries?

Out of the list of "laying down requirements" above, which do you find you relate to most in your life? I will share that mine is, "friction with others of its kind." I can't stand to have friction with a fellow sheep; I tend to want to bend over backwards to get others to like me. Women can be especially mean and I have had to often learn the hard way that not all of them will think I am wonderful.

Please share and explain the "laying down requirement" that you relate most with below.

It seems that there is no way to escape from the torments of simply being alive in this fallen world; however, that is exactly why Christ came. It is only after we enter His pasture that we can truly find rest.

Read Matthew 11:28-30 and record below a summary of what Christ is saying.

Christ said these words right after He rebuked some of the cities where He had shared the good news of His coming. He even provided miracles for the people to display the authenticity of His message, and yet the people had not believed in Him or repented. Christ was directing these rebukes to those who "knew," yet did not "respond." The Great Shepherd revealed Himself to these people, yet they chose not to look and see Him. In turning away, perhaps they felt that they might avoid having to respond to His revelation.

In Matthew 11:25-26, Christ is saying a prayer. What does His prayer reveal about who will gain the "revelation" in God's kingdom and who will not?

My four-year-old little girl has the most beautiful hair, however it seems that each morning she wakes up with a tennis ball size tangle right in the back of her head. The first time I had to work that tangle out of her hair was more painful for me, I think, than it was for her. I had to chase her around the house with a brush as she ran from me crying and holding her hands over her head. I know it hurts her when I have to work these tangles out, but I love her too much to let her go out in to the world looking like a mess. Eventually, she came to understand that I am going to get those tangles out no matter what, so she stopped fighting me about it. I don't think she understands yet why I have to do it, but she understands that I am going to do it no matter how much she protests. It tenders my heart now each morning when she willingly comes to me and stands to let me work her tangles out, even when it hurts.

Our Shepherd, Christ, wants us to trust Him enough to be like His little children, willingly standing there with Him as He untangles us from the effects of sin and pain in our lives. We don't always know why He does what He does, why He leads us through some of the places that He must, or why He permits such harm when He has the power to stop it. So often, like sheep, we refuse to lie down and rest in the pastures that He has provided because we think that as long as we struggle and strive, we at least have some control over our destiny. We hang onto this world for dear life, not realizing that we are only one surrender away from entering into green pastures with Him. We can't see that His purpose is for our greater good, and that only He knows what it will take for us not to walk around in this world looking like a mess. So often it takes the heaviest burdens in life to "*make* us lie down" in the green pastures, and once we look up, we realize that our escape from our burdens was never on Earth, but in Himself, where our Shepherd is always leading us.

Have you recently experienced The Shepherd *making* you lie down in green pastures?" If so, please explain below.

Please complete the following sentence based on what you have learned today, "If He makes me lie down in green pastures (based on Psalm 23:2),

_____

_____

Great job, you are becoming more Ewe already!

Day 3

The LORD is my Shepherd
"He leads me beside still waters"

<table>
<tr>
<td>DAILY
GRAIN
</td>
<td>Please begin by prayerfully receiving God's Word to you through these Scripture(s):

"He leads me beside the still waters." Psalm 23:3a

"Deep calls to deep at the roar of your waterfalls; all your breakers and your waves have gone over me." Psalm 42:7</td>
</tr>
</table>

My family and I recently returned from a vacation where we stayed right on the banks of a major river. Our hopes of getting to ride the river were dashed once we discovered that our youngest daughter was not old enough to take part in a raft ride on the river. The only river ride we were able to partake of this year was the lazy river at our resort. At first I was annoyed; I looked forward to this trip, in part, because it would have been my first real river adventure with my family. We have been on the theme park river rides that were designed to *feel* real, but never before had we experienced sitting on the raging waters, not knowing what was right around the next bend. One evening as I drifted on the smooth waters of the lazy river, gazing at the stars above, I heard God's voice whisper a reminder of this Psalm, "He leads me beside the still waters." Tears filled my eyes as I looked back over my life and was able to catch a glimpse of all the ways my Shepherd has guided me out of the danger of the raging rivers in my life and into the security of His still waters.

What about you? Does your life experience at this point feel more like a ride on a raging river or have you been experiencing a smooth ride on the still waters?

I am the oldest daughter out of five children born to a single mother. We lived in poverty as I was growing up. Due to my mother's constant need to work to support us, I was often neglected and became easy prey for abusers of all types. The raging rivers of life, confusion, rejection, and pain had already begun to overwhelm me before I even started kindergarten. My childhood became a chaotic quest for survival. I learned to grab hold of any life raft anyone would toss me, even if it hurt to hold on. I tried hiding from the waves, perhaps if they did not see me, they might stop taking me under. Like David in the 42nd Psalm, I found early on that the deep seemed to call out to me, that the breakers and waves were constantly going right over me. After a while, I learned to stop looking for life rafts, to harden my heart, swallow my pain, and just succumb to the raging waters. Ironically, the waves rolling over me became my security and roars of the raging waters, my lullaby. Somehow, my heart had stopped craving the warmth and security of the still waters. I stopped longing for them and began my destructive descent into the darkness of the deep.

Although I cannot remember a time when I did not sense Jesus in my life, it was not until I was thirty that I began to understand just why He had come. Even in the raging waters, I could sense Him right there in the waves with me. Even when I let myself go into the depths, I could sense His heart calling out to me. At the age of thirty, I was pregnant with my second child, Faith. Just like my mother, I was a single mom who was merely trying to survive. However, something in my heart was breaking as I contemplated the lives that I was now bringing in to the world. I could already see that my son, Joshua, was now experiencing the fear and terror that comes with being thrown into the raging waters without a life raft. Although I hated it and wanted so badly to become his life raft, I did not know how. I had already drowned and accepted it, but as I watched him go under and knew that my little girl would have to endure the same, I was broken in such a way that I was not sure how to recover. I was either going to die or finally learn how to live. It was then that the awareness of Christ, the one that had never left me, but that I had silenced with my own bitterness, became like a lifejacket for me. I was going to wrap Him all around me and pray that He would bring me to the surface again so that I could help my children.

And He did. He took my hand and led right to the still waters of His Presence. My problem now was that, in my flesh, I had learned to feel safer in the raging rivers of life than the still waters of Christ's Presence. Could I begin to embrace and trust these still waters? That is the question of a lifetime.

What about you? Take a moment and pray. Ask God to show you the truth about yourself and your life. Is it a raging river (maybe not in the same way as mine was), or are you learning to find life in His still waters? Explain.

Sometimes our raging rivers take on the form of a life that is out of control in very well meaning ways. The captivity of activity is one of this world's deadliest raging rivers and is so deceptive in its traps. It calls out to you, "You are not enough, your kids are not enough. Do more, become more, and then maybe the world will embrace you." Like hamsters in a wheel, we run and run, feeling the work of it, just sure that we are getting somewhere, but never arriving. We are not saved until we step out of the wheel and look to the Shepherd to lead us to real life.

In what ways might you be struggling right now with "the captivity of activity?"

Take a moment now and ask Christ to help you step out of your wheel and lead you to real life.

So often we are afraid to leave our wheels behind because our wheels are tangible. They represent something that does not exist in some spiritual domain, but exists here on Earth, where we somewhat know how to function and survive. However, if we truly belong to Christ, we are no longer of this world. We do not belong in the wheel anymore because the wheel is tied to a world that is not ours. As long as we are in that wheel, we—and our loved ones who we influence—will gain no true ground in God's kingdom. When are we going to begin caring more about gaining ground in Christ than about becoming something in this world? One day, this whole world will pass away and all that will exist is Christ's kingdom. I want to have something to claim there, in that moment when all that is temporary has fallen under the weight of all that is eternal. Don't you?

What about you? In what ways do you tend to strive for what is temporary over what is eternal?

Look up the following Scriptures and record below what they say about this world. Record any new insight that God is showing you from these Scriptures.

Matthew 16:24-26

John 12:46

John 15:18-19

Romans 12:1-2

1 John 2:15-17

Our Shepherd longs to lead you beside the still waters, Sweet One. He loves you too much to watch you get tossed back and forth in the raging waters of this world. "I have told you these things, so that in me you may have peace. In this world you will have trouble. But take heart! I have overcome the world." (John 16:33). Still waters do not exist here on Earth, except in the hearts of those who bathe in the peace-filled waters of Christ. He wants to lead you there because, once you are His, it is the only place you truly belong.

Please close in a prayer of gratitude for His peace filled waters. Great job, Little Lamb!

Day 4

The LORD is my Shepherd
"He restores my soul"

DAILY GRAIN	Please begin by prayerfully receiving God's Word to you through these Scriptures: *"He restores my soul" Psalm 23:3(b)* *"Out of the anguish of his soul he shall see and be satisfied; by his knowledge shall the righteous one, my servant, make many to be accounted righteous, and he shall bear their iniquities." Isaiah 53:11*

I have the most exquisite nativity set that I received as a gift from my mom five years ago. It was always our greatest joy to place it out in our home to mark the beginning of the Christmas season for us. Last year as I was packing away all of our Christmas décor, I just could not bear to pack the nativity away. I just love it too much. What began as a procrastination has now become part of our homes everyday décor. If you come in to my home, you will see our amazing nativity set right there in our living room, even as you pant for the coolness of A/C as you seek escape from the Texas heat in the middle of July. Of course, when I made this decision (or in my case, refused to make the decision), I did not think about how the exposure to everyday life in the de la Moriniere home might "enhance" this precious heirloom of ours. There are too many stories to tell about the adventures that our shepherds, wise-men, sheep, and even baby Jesus have seen. I can just tell you that super glue does work in gluing baby Jesus' head back on, that sheep can still stand on three feet, and can even look pretty decent after an ear has been broken off. I can tell you that Christ has used those broken lambs to speak in to my heart so much more than He ever did when they were all nice and put together. He never ceases to amaze me with all of the ways He breaks through to our hearts. What I thought was this exquisite décor to our home, He has broken apart and used to show me more about how exquisite His own heart truly is. I will never forget the day I came home to find one of my fragile lambs being carried in the mouth of our family dog. I panicked at the thought that he could drop it onto the hardwood floor at any moment and it would be shattered and impossible to put back together. As I cautiously removed my precious lamb from his mouth, I could sense God's presence reminding me of the day that He had to take the lifeless body of His Son, our Lamb, out of the mouth of the wolf that had devoured Him. My heart still breaks at the thought of that sacrifice. We will never know just how much "breaking" it took for our sins to have been paid for. He died so that we might never fully know what real death is.

Through this study so far, we have been reflecting on knowing Christ as our Shepherd, but today's lesson will depart from that aspect of Christ's character and move more towards knowing Him as our Lamb, the sacrifice given up for us.

> Just to get us started, what do you know about lambs so far (if anything)? Please record your knowledge of lambs below.

Isaiah 53 gives us a clear picture of Christ as our Lamb. Please read all of it and answer the questions below.

> Based on verses 2-3, what was Christ's experience on Earth like? What was He like?

> Can you relate in any way to His earthly experience?

Based on verse 5, please personalize this verse by filling your name in the blanks below:

"But he was wounded for _____'s transgressions; he was crushed for _____'s iniquities; upon him was the chastisement that brought _____ peace, and with his stripes _____ is healed.

Please read and reflect upon the verse above and record any responses that you have to it below.

According to verse 6, who has gone astray?

Verses 7-9 speak volumes about how Christ responded to His affliction and sacrifice. Record below some of the adjectives that describe Him.

I wonder if you noticed that many of the adjectives listed above have to do with Christ's mouth, His silence, His unwillingness to complain about what He was enduring. So many times, our mouths give away the true intentions of our hearts.

Based on Christ's actions (or lack thereof), what can you determine about His true intentions?

Please record below how you often respond when oppressed, judged, afflicted or cut off?

According to verses 10-11, whose will was it to crush Christ, and for what reason was it His will?

According to Leviticus 1, when the Israelites would go to the tabernacle to make an offering and sacrifice to the Lord, the sacrifice had to be a male, and without blemish. These lambs were often set apart from birth and given special attention by the family that they belonged to, often treated as beloved pets. At the time for atonement, the person (most often the father of the family) making the sacrifice would bring his lamb to the tabernacle, stand at the tent entrance and place his hand on the head of the lamb that was to be slain. This was seen as a sign of transfer of sin from the man on to the animal (the atonement). As the lamb is killed and its blood drained, the owner's hand can feel the life literally leaving the animal. In the case of sheep, they are typically very timid animals and do not make a sound as they give up their lives as an offering for sin. I can picture in my mind the big, black, innocent eyes of the lamb just staring in up in to the face of its owner, not knowing that right there, in that very moment, its whole purpose for coming to life was being fulfilled. Just as our Lamb's was, the destiny of these blameless and spotless lambs was to die for the sins of his people.

According to verse 12, what will the transgressors receive through Christ's sacrifice and victory?

Just as the hands of the sinners needing atonement grasped the head of the innocent lamb that was to be slain, we who are sinners grasp the head of our Lamb as we enter into the freedom that comes once we are ransomed from our sins. To embrace this grace, we must first walk through the blood. Like broken lambs in need of super glue to get us back together, we enter in and His blood makes all things new. Jesus always loves us broken lambs best and, just like my nativity lambs, He speaks to us most when we come to Him broken. " ...Those who are well have no need of a physician, but those who are sick ... For I came not for the righteous, but for the sinners." (Matthew 9:12-13). To fix broken lambs is the whole reason Christ, our Shepherd, came.

Have you ever come to that place where you are willingly ready to come to Christ and admit your brokenness? If so, please share. If not, why not do it now?

Please close in prayer sharing what is on your heart today with your Lamb. Let the super glue of His blood wash over you and put you all back together again.

Rejection

Rejection…. It is a word that all of us can relate to.

Sometimes it may be difficult to picture God is being one who actually became aquainted with rejection. However, Isaiah 53:3 assures us, *"He was despised and rejected by men; a man of sorrows, and acquainted with grief, and as one from whom men hide their faces, he was despised, and we esteemed him not."*

We often miss out on the broader view of this verse by ascribing it only to what Jesus experienced at the Cross. As we take a deeper look into His Word, we can see that this verse proves true, Jesus was misunderstood, underestimated, undervalued, and above all else *Rejected.* Let's spend some time on each of these words…letting our experience mold together with His.

Beside each word, write an experience that first comes to mind in your own life. Spend time in prayer with Jesus in that experience and letting Him meet you there. Thank-Him for being with you there.

DESPISED

REJECTED

SORROW

ASHAMED OF

NOT ESTEEMED

I wish I were there to hug you, cry with you or even maybe laugh with you (or both) over what you wrote above. I know that our journey as woman walking with Jesus is anything but boring, and unfortunately it is so often painful. I wish I wasn't painful or that we didn't have to experience rejection (especially in the body of Christ). However, we are not home yet, we are all still BECOMING , hence the need for AMAZING GRACE. But we can take great comfort in knowing that our beautiful Shepherd was the only one who ever experienced COMPLETE rejection, from both heaven and earth. None of us will ever know what that was like.

Beloved, even at those moments when it has seemed that everyone with skin on has turned away from you, Jesus hasn't. He literally had His skin torn off to nail it down once and for all, that HE WILL NEVER LEAVE YOU! You are HIS! And you are LOVED.

Day 5

The LORD is my Shepherd
"He leads me in paths of righteousness
for His name's sake"

DAILY GRAIN	Please begin by prayerfully receiving God's Word to you through these Scriptures:
	"He leads me in paths of righteousness for His name's sake" Psalm 23:3(c)
	"But now thus says the LORD, he who created you, O Jacob, he who formed you, O Israel: 'Fear not, for I have redeemed you; I have called you by name, you are mine." Isaiah 43:1

As I began wring this study, there is one song that seemed to never leave my mind. "Mary had a little lamb, little lamb, little lamb, Mary had a little lamb, whose fleece was white as snow … and everywhere that Mary went that lamb was sure to go."

Of course I am sure that you can relate. However, as crazy as this sounds, there is some deep theological truth that can be found by looking in to this nursery rhyme. As we discovered yesterday, we do have a Lamb who not only has a fleece as "white as snow," but one who also has made yours and mine, "as white as snow" too. All throughout Scripture, more specifically in Hebrews 13:5, we are promised by Christ that, "I will never leave you or forsake you." So, yes, we can say with confidence that "everywhere that

Mary (and the rest of us) goes, that *Lamb* is sure to go." I shared part of my testimony with you earlier this week about how I always sensed Christ in my life, but never really began knowing Him until I was thirty. I truly believe that *knowing* Him has everything to do with who is the one following and who is the one trying to lead. Just as a shepherd must guide his sheep in the direction he knows in advance is best for them to go, we must trust our Shepherd to guide us in the direction that He knows is best for us to go. This sounds so simple, but we sheep are so prone to wander, so prone to want to be the shepherd, that we become a *you* instead of an *ewe*.

In Deuteronomy 30:11-20, Moses is giving God's people some last instructions before they enter into the Promised Land. He led these people for forty years through a wilderness where the people were forced to learn how to be shepherded by God Himself. God led them during this time through the very tangible means of a cloud by day and a pillar of fire by night.

Please read Deuteronomy 30:11-20 and then answer the questions below.

According to verses 11-14, how available is God's instruction to us?

In verses 15-19, what two options is God laying before His people?

In verse 16, what does God say will it take for the people to choose life?

In verse 17-18, what can happen to cause the people to inherit death?

What does verse 17 say can be "turned away" and what does this have to do with "hearing?"

James 1:13-15 speaks to how we easily can "turn away" in our hearts.

"Let no one say when he is tempted, 'I am being tempted by God' for God cannot be tempted with evil, and he himself tempts no one. But each person is tempted when he is lured and enticed by his own desire. Then desire when it has conceived gives birth to sin, and sin when it is fully grown brings forth death."

According to the verse above, how is one "enticed?"

What does this say about our natural desires? Do our desires tend to lead us towards life or death?

According to Deuteronomy 30:19, what does God wish for us to choose?

He states in this verse that another group is affected by what our choices are, who are they? How does this impact you?

This one really hits home with me, for I have seen with own eyes the ramifications that my sinful choices have had on my children. How I want to choose life, not only for myself, but even more so for them.

In verse 20, there are three actions given that can keep us in "life." Please list them below.

My favorite part of this whole passage is in verse 20 where, after we are given the instructions above, we are told, "for **he is your life** and length of days"(emphasis mine). It is so easy for us to think that we don't truly have to be intentional about walking with God. We think we can coast for a while and that there is a rest stop where we can sit and prop up our feet. In reality, there is life and death, and whether we choose to believe it or not, we are headed in only one of those directions at any time. Not only that, but we are leading those who follow us in one of those directions with us.

Every time we depart from choosing life, our Lamb calls out to us, trying to woo us back to Himself. He doesn't do this because He wants to be in control, but because He is life! With His own life He paid the price for every single step we take on the shores of death. Love does not exist without the element of choice in whether to express it or not. Love paid the price for our entire journey. It is up to us to decide if we will walk in it.

> So often, our perception of Christ is skewed by our own sin nature. We confuse grace with permission, Christ's mercy with blindness, and Christ's longing to shepherd us with his willingness to let us become our own shepherds. We sing the song, "Everywhere that we go, that Lamb is sure to go." However, we forget that our Lamb already went. His choice for us was sealed before any of us were even born. Each day, He is looking for *our choice*. Will we be His, or will we belong to the world? Will we be the sheep of His pasture or will we go out and try to be our own shepherds?

In all honesty, what is your typical choice? Do you let yourself belong to Him or do you seek to become your own shepherd?

Out of the whole Bible, the words in Isaiah 43 are my very favorite. As a girl who grew up without a daddy, I have always longed more than anything to "belong" to someone who would protect me. I will never forget the day that I heard the Lord pronounce over me, "You are mine!" I still get tears in my eyes as I think about it.

> Like me, have you longed to belong to someone? At the same time, is there a fear that prohibits you from choosing to accept this "belonging?" Please share below.

We will finish our lesson today contemplating Isaiah 43:1-11. Please answer the following questions after reading over the verses.

> In verse 2, where does God say He will go with us?

> In verse 7, what are the three ways God describes His children?

> In verse 10, the Lord is giving us some insight into His purposes for us. What can you determine are His purposes for us based on this verse?

We sheep are very nearsighted; however, we are God's chosen instruments to carry out His purposes for His glory. He just gets a kick out of using the weakest and most dependent of all to carry His greatest message in to the world. "He leads us through paths of righteousness for His names sake." What a blessing it is to be the ones He has chosen to carry the banner of Christ's love in to this world.

So often we turn away in fear or complacency from this great task. We fear not being successful so we never even try. However, Christ never asks us for great success: He asks us for our obedience and faith in Him. When we take up Christ's cause, we never have to fear failure because victory has already been won. All we do is extend Christ's victory further and further into our own lives and, in doing so, touch others with His love. "For his names sake," we choose to walk one more step each moment.

> "Remember not the former things, nor consider the things of old. Behold, I am doing a new thing; now it springs forth, do you not perceive it? I will make a way in the wilderness and rivers in the desert" Isaiah 43:18-19. Sweet lamb, only He can lead us through this wilderness of life and, in the midst of it all, provide newness each day. In closing, please share if there is anything new He is causing you to become aware of in your life?

Please close in a prayer of gratitude for the loving Shepherd that He is. You have done a wonderful job this week. I am so honored to be on this journey with you.

Week 2

Will You Become One With Jesus?

Fill in the blanks below with the words according to the lesson:
one, identity, security, love, needs, you, purpose

Romans 6:19, *"I am speaking in human terms, because of your natural limitations. For just as you once presented your members as slaves to impurity and to lawlessness leading to more lawlessness, so now present your members to slaves to righteousness leading to sanctification."*

God is asking me, "Do you really _____ Me? Are you _____ with Me?"

The enemy always comes after our _____.

Ways we are tempted just as Jesus was:

1. God won't provide for my _____.

2. God won't provide for my _____.

3. God won't provide for my _____.

_____ are the Bride of Christ!

Notes_____

_____

_____

_____

_____

_____

Day 1

The Valley of the Shadow of Death

DAILY GRAIN	Please begin by prayerfully receiving God's Word to you through these Scriptures: *"Even though I walk through the valley of the shadow of death," Psalm 23:4 (a)* *"For this perishable body must put on the imperishable, and this mortal body must put on immortality. When the perishable puts on the imperishable, and the mortal puts on immortality, then shall come to pass the saying that is written:* *'Death is swallowed up in victory.' O death, where is your victory? O death, where is your sting?'" 1 Corinthians 15:53-55*

I had forgotten that kind of sorrow until I recognized it again in her face. "Mommy, why did he die?," was all I could make out between the shallow breaths and the uncontrollable sobs. The sight of her crinkled up, pink, and puffy face alone was enough to bring any parent to her knees. It was my precious Faith, my eight-year old daughter, and she was asking the question that all of us wish we could answer. Children have a way of bringing such honesty in to a situation that it awakens those places in our hearts that we had all but forgotten were there. As I held my heartbroken daughter, I felt my own heart breaking as the realization flooded through me that I cannot shield my babies from the brutality and finality of death. Sooner or later, we are all wounded by its grasp. However, in Christ, there is a hope that exists beyond death. To catch a glimpse of the hope, we must also walk through the valley with Him. This is one of the pinnacle portions of our study so we will spend two days on this lesson as we contemplate both the hope and the sorrow that exists in the valley of the shadow of death.

As I contemplated how to write about such a comprehensive subject, I came to meet someone along the way who blessed me with an awareness of both the beauty and sorrow of death. I just knew he was the one to help us walk through this portion of the study. His name is Joey, and he is a lamb that I met while reading to prepare for this study. He lives in a book called, *Heaven has Blue Carpet,* and I cannot wait for you to meet him. I would highly recommend reading this book if you would like to understand more about the aspects of the relationship that exists between a shepherd and his(or her) sheep. Joey was born on a winter night to a mother who rejected him. He was lucky enough to belong to a wonderful (although inexperienced at this point) shepherd. This first excerpt explains the circumstances around his birth and how he ended up in the home of his shepherd.

"By now the little guy was all hunched over. His head was hanging so low I thought there might be something wrong with his neck, but it was his spirit. We didn't realize this little guy had been getting wounded every time his mom gave him the thumbs- down refusal, and now "rejection personified." Then he started shivering, and when he clamped his dry mouth shut and wouldn't even lick the milk I was squirting at him, I knew he had given up. "I'm bringing him into the house now. We will give him a house full of mothers and a dad to boot." Everyone clapped and hooted, and our youngest daughter yelled between sobs, "We'll take you to our house, and you'll be ours forever and ever!'" (Heaven Has Blue Carpet, pg 41).

"After this, Jesus, knowing that all was now finished, said, 'I thirst." John 19:28

"If the world hates you, know that it has hated me before it hated you. If you were of the world, the world would love you as its own; but because you are not of the world, but I chose you out of the world, therefore the world hates you." John 17:18-19

"Just so, I tell you, there is joy before the angels over one sinner who repents." Luke 15:10

There is something so amazing about the mystery of how God uses all things to make us His own. He shepherds us to some of the highest mountains only to prepare us for the greatest valleys. He led the Israelites out of Egypt and allowed them to experience the mountaintop miracle of parting the waters of the Red Sea; however, He also led them through the wilderness for forty years as He allowed them to endure the valleys of thirst, hunger, fear, exhaustion, disappointment and even death as He revealed to His people the miracle of Himself. As little lambs, some of us may have wondered how our "good" Shepherd could have allowed some of what we have gone through to occur. However, just like little Joey, sometimes it is the world's rejection that opens the door to our hearts to an experience that is bigger than what we could have ever imagined. "He came to his own, and his own people did not receive him. But to all who did receive him, who believed in his name, he gave the right to become children of God, who were born, not of blood, not of the will of flesh nor of the will of man, but of God," (John 1:12-13). Sister, if you belong to Christ, you do not belong to this world; you are God's kid and can only experience true belonging in His arms. To experience the rejection of this world is to identify with Christ's own rejection. Like Him, you were born not to belong here on Earth, but to bring to Earth a sense of what it is to belong to Heaven. Like Him, we are here not to show the world how to live, but to show the world what it is to die and be resurrected to a life that is not of this world. As Matthew 10:39 says, "Whoever finds his life will lose it, and whoever loses his life for [Christ's] sake will find it." We are here to lose our lives for Christ sake, for without Him life does not exist.

> What about you? Do you tend to feel more at home here on Earth or do you sometimes feel more like an alien here? Please explain below.

Please look up the following verses and record below how they either confirm your earthly experience or challenge what you are experiencing.

> Romans 6:1-7

> Galatians 2:20

> 1 Corinthians 6:19-20

"For this perishable body must put on the imperishable, and this mortal body must put on immortality. When the perishable puts on the imperishable, and the mortal puts on immortality, then shall come to pass the saying that is written:

'Death is swallowed up in victory.' O death, where is your victory? O death, where is your sting?'" 1 Corinthians 15:53-55

Just as Joey had to lay aside his hope for a life out in the barn with his mother and the other lambs, we are to lay aside ours for true life in Christ. Perhaps, if we are truly honest with ourselves and each other, we will acknowledge that it is our pain, our inability, and our brokenness in this world that first brought us to the Savior or is bringing us to Him now. Let's face it: if life stayed easy for us here, we might never willingly leave the comfort of our own pastures to follow our Shepherd.

> Take a moment here and record what it is that first brought you to or is bringing you now to the Shepherd?

> Are there aspects of walking with your Shepherd through this valley that make you afraid? If so, please share them.

Some of us need to get on with dying so that we can get on with living. So often we try to hold on so tight and so hard to our personal interpretations of life, not realizing that we were never here to "hold on" to life, but were created to let go until there is nothing left to let go of. That is when we discover that life has been waiting there for us all along. Under all of our wool is the treasure and adventure of true life, life that is not based on our personal interpretations, but on life itself, the literal breath of God.

> Have you ever really thought about your own definition of life? Without looking at a dictionary, define life.

Are you willing to admit that you might not truly know what life is? If so, let's take a moment here and pray for God to show us. Initial here after you have prayed_____.

Let's take one more look at our little lamb, Joey, as he has now left life out in the pasture to enter into his shepherd's care.

"Joey was brought into our home and experienced things that were unbelievable to the other residents of Sheep World. No barn straw for Joey-he was living on the soft, luxurious blue carpet that was throughout his master's house. Joey was rocked to sleep, watched cartoons with Ann and Jimmy, rode in the car with Lynn, was covered with kisses, wrapped in flannel blankets, and became the center of attention with every visitor … Little Joey just snuggled up in everyone's neck and would have purred (if lambs could). "No eye has seen, no ear has heard, no mind conceived what God has prepared for those who love him." (1 Corinthians 2:9). Joey would have been called a bummer lamb by the sheep industry because most shepherds considered these orphans a nuisance. I now believe the bummers are the winners. Who in all of Sheep World experienced a taste of heaven? Our little bummer, Joey. Who took naps on soft carpet? Joey. Who was personally cared for by the shepherd and his family? Joey. Because Joey *chose* to live and *allowed* us to love him, he became the most blessed lamb in our entire flock!" (Heaven Has Blue Carpet, pg. 50-51).

Are there aspects of your life that sometimes lead you to believe that your life is a "bummer?" If so, what are they? Please share them below.

Perhaps, it is our sheep-like nature that causes us to look for the "bummers" in life instead of the blessings of life lived out on the blue carpet of Heaven. Are there ways that you are experiencing your Shepherd's care right now?

If not, please pray for the Lord to open your eyes to see all of the ways He is shepherding you right now. He longs for His sheep and longs to lavish you in His loving care.

Please close in a prayer thanking our Shepherd for walking with us through this valley of the shadow of death so that we might find true life right on the other side of it.

Day 2

The Valley of the Shadow of Death

DAILY
GRAIN

Please begin by prayerfully receiving God's Word to you through these Scriptures:

"Even though I walk through the valley of the shadow of death, I will fear no evil " Psalm 23:4 (b)

"He was oppressed, and he was afflicted, yet he opened not his mouth; like a lamb that is led to slaughter, and like a sheep before its shearers is silent, so he opened not his mouth." Isaiah 53:7

As I sit here now writing this, my four year old, Hope, is coloring pictures next to me and singing in the sweetest, little voice. She is singing a song that we probably all know, "He's got the whole world in his hands, He's got the whole world in his hands, He's got the whole world in his hands …" My familiarity with the song almost kept me from noticing that her words have changed as she moves from, "He's got the whole world in his hands," to, "He's got the whole wicked in his hands, He's got the whole wicked in his hands, He's got the whole wicked in his hands." My heart is touched by all the ways our God and Shepherd uses everything to teach us the simplicity of what it is to follow Him.

The truth is that our Shepherd does have the whole world, as well as all of the wickedness in it in His hands. We are reminded in Psalm 37:23-24 that every step we take lies in His powerful hands, "The steps of a man are established by the LORD, when he delights in his way; though he fall, he shall not be cast headlong, for the LORD upholds his hand."

We spent yesterday looking into how we must walk through the valley of the shadow of death with our Shepherd in order to truly come to life. Today we will walk through the valley of the shadow of death with Christ as we contemplate His own journey through the reality of death so that we would never have to know anything but its shadow. Webster's dictionary defines shadow as, "an area that is not or is only partially irradiated or illuminated because of the interception of radiation by an opaque object between the area and the source of radiation, the rough image cast by an object blocking rays of illumination, or an imperfect imitation or copy."

As we can see, a shadow can only be formed when an object intercepts something from a source of radiation. Over 2,000 years ago, Christ stood in the way of death getting to us; therefore, we will never even know what death truly is. He blocked it from us so that a shadow of it is all we will ever know. If we could catch a glance from the mountaintop and see the image of the shadow covering over us through the valley, we would see that it would take the form of a cross. Galatians 5:24-25 says, "And those who belong to Christ Jesus have crucified the flesh with its passions and desires. If we live by the Spirit, let us also walk by the Spirit." When Christ calls out to us to, "pick up our cross and follow Him," (Luke 9:23) it is because He wants us to know Him. The Shepherd is calling out to His sheep, "Come and walk with Me, know Me, trust Me." It is in this valley where our knowledge and trust for our Shepherd is most tested and refined. The valley is where we truly learn to depend on and follow our good Shepherd and where the words of 1ˢᵗ Corinthians 15:53-55 leap from the pages of our Bibles to the reality of our lives, "'Death is swallowed up in victory.' O death, where is your victory? O death, where is your sting?'"

> How about you? In what ways has the fear of death kept you from fully entering in to the journey with Christ?

> How does knowing that we will never have to walk through the true reality of death change your perception of it?

I have a friend who passed away two years ago from cancer, leaving behind two young daughters and a devoted family. As she "fought the good fight," I could sense her struggling to know whether to continue fighting or to prepare for what it looked like was coming. I prayed for her so often and begged God not to take her when she still had so many who needed her. It was only after she passed away that the awareness of the gift of life and the influence we are given in it began to sink in. I have always viewed it as having a beginning and an end, with the beginning being my birth and the end being my death either from some disease, old age, or some other tragedy. However, through the miracle of God's Word, Christ is showing me that He *is* the newness of my beginning as well as the mercy of my end. He is life, and by His grace, He has extended me an invitation to join Him in the miracle of His presence. Who am I to fear? What can man do to me? I am alive in Christ!

Let's look up some Scriptures together to help us grasp the freedom in this knowledge. Look up the following Scriptures and record your insight about them below.

> Colossians 3:1-4

> Revelation 21:5-7

> Revelation 22:1-5

Okay, by now I am sure you are wondering if we are ever going to find out more about our little friend, Joey. Well, I was saving the best for now. As Joey grew, his mother, the shepherd, began to notice his need to spend time with the other lambs in the pasture. Below are her observations of him after he was turned out to pasture.

"As time went on, it was obvious that security was written all over Joey. He emanated an inner confidence that enabled him to walk fearlessly among the defensive ewes. He walked through their ranks oblivious to the butts and angry baas and was unaffected by their brutality. He carried himself with a regal demeanor never seen before in Sheep World. He appeared to be alone, but he wasn't. Our love was always with him. Joey didn't have a sheep father or mother, brother, or sister, but he knew he had more. The owner and master of all the sheep in Sheep World adopted him."

"But we also rejoice in our sufferings, because sufferings produce perseverance, perseverance, character, and character, hope. And hope does not disappoint us, because God has poured out his love into our hearts by the Holy Spirit, whom he has given us. (Romans 5:3-5)" (Heaven Has Blue Carpet, pg. 59).

Only in Christ can we exude the confidence in this world that comes with living a fearless life. Not a life that excludes fearsome circumstances, but a life that knows that nothing can get to us without having to go through our Shepherd first.

Are there aspects of life that cause you to feel as if you are being "butted" by this world?

What are your biggest fears in life?

Let's take a moment right here to pray and ask God for a new confidence in His ability to shepherd us in this world.

"Lord, I must admit that there are things in this world that fill me with unspeakable fear. I admit to you, Father, that I am afraid of death and of how it has the potential to take me away from those I love or those I love away from me. However Lord, I want to live a fearless life. I don't want to be afraid of walking through the valley of the shadow of death with you. Please plant eternity so strongly in my heart that not even death can keep me from living fearlessly for You. I want to experience the freedom that You died to give us. Please help me to get there. Amen."

Did you find it challenging to pray the prayer above? If so, why? What are you experiencing right now? If you did not, what do you think is prohibiting you from praying it? Please share below.

"Now that Joey was on grain, I was able to wean him from the bottle. He wasn't my baby anymore; he was growing up and living his whole life in Sheep World now. He continued to stand out from the other sheep as an out-of-the ordinary, rare, set-apart young ram. Why was he different? What set him apart?

Instead of spending his whole life seeking after food, as the rest of the flock did, he was spending it seeking after me, his food-giver, his shepherd." (Heaven Has Blue Carpet, pg.61-62).

I can't help but think of another fellow sheep as I contemplate our little lamb, Joey. His name is Enoch, and you can meet him in Genesis 5:15-27. Please meet me there and answer the following questions below.

What do verses 22-24 say about Enoch?

Enoch walked with God, and then he was not, for God took him. Once we are in Christ, all of our lives are just a long walk home with God. A journey from *you* to *ewe*, that is the destination.

I love how in the middle of all of these genealogies, there is this pause, where God takes notice of a lamb that is willing to walk with Him. The Lord searches all over the Earth looking for one who is willing to walk with Him, to care more about intimacy with Him than arriving at an earthly destination. Our journey is our destiny. Just as Christ's destiny was the cross, all of our lives involve a destiny that walks us through the valley of the shadow of death until all that has represented death in us is no more, for God has taken us.

> Joey was willing to walk with his shepherd, and because he did, his life meant something more, not only to his shepherd, but to each of us who know his story. If God can use an orphan lamb to bring Him glory, than how much more can He use us?

"Then how can you do it, Mom? How can you take him to be ..." "Because I love the little guy, that's how. To keep him would be fun for us but not for Joey. After all he's been through, he deserves to come into his destiny." (Heaven Has Blue Carpet, pg. 73).

"Without speaking, we guided our immaculate, pampered lambs through the now pig-stenched aisleway and into one of the prison-like cells, I mean, stalls. The lambs were packed together like sardines and didn't move or make a sound. Their silence endeared them to me ... which made me feel worse. They were so innocent.

We were ready to leave when we heard a little commotion. A lamb from the rear was pushing and shoving his way to the front. I was afraid to look. Sure enough, it was Joey. He looked me straight in the eye and didn't make a sound. I looked into his beautiful face and held his head with both of my hands and told him for the last time, "It's going to be okay, little guy." (Heaven Has Blue Carpet, pg. 75).

"He was oppressed, and he was afflicted, yet he opened not his mouth; like a lamb that is led to slaughter, and like a sheep before its shearers is silent, so he opened not his mouth." Isaiah 53:7

"Precious in the sight of the Lord is the death of his saints." Psalm 116:15

"When Jesus had received the sour wine, he said, "It is finished," and he bowed his head and gave up his spirit." John 19:30

Ladies, your Shepherd really does have the "whole world in His hands." His bloody hands stretched from east to west on a cross declaring to all the universe, "I've got the whole wicked in My hands, you are safe now little lambs, even in the valley of the shadow of death."

Please close by thanking our Lamb for the victory over death that we have in Him.

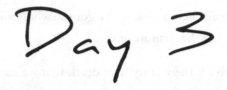

The Valley of the Shadow of Death

DAILY GRAIN	Please begin by prayerfully receiving God's Word to you through these Scriptures: *"...I will fear no evil, for you are with me; ..." Psalm 23:4(b)* *"The Word became flesh and blood, and moved into the neighborhood ..." John 1:14(a) The Message*

I had no idea what actually happened the day I married my husband. Even as I stood there giddy and giggly, taking the vows of a lifetime, the loudness of every eye in the building on me was so much bigger than my own voice repeating the sacred vows that moved me from being Rhonda to Matt's wife. Like so many of us when we come to Christ, I had no idea that I had become something that I did not know how to be. Even during our honeymoon, I was still oblivious to the weight of what had just happened to me. I felt like a little kid at the 4th of July, waiting for my bottle rocket to go off, waiting for the explosion to occur in my own consciousness that I had become something completely new. It was not until about two weeks later that any semblance of this transformation began to hit home. All of the wedding hoopla was over with. I was back at work and my life was pretty much back to normal. Since my son, Josh, was already secure in his elementary school, Matt and I had decided that it would be best for him to move into our house. After work one day, I stepped through our front door to find that my new husband had moved his furniture into *our* house. That is when it finally hit me. I will never forget the feeling that swept over me as I saw that his world had descended on to mine. His dad had helped with the move and was resting on my new husband's sofa in the front room. As I walked past, I realized that he was not only Matt's dad, but he had become my dad, too. There was a *real* dad sitting in my living room on my *real* husband's furniture. And they were both mine! How did this happen, Lord? Thank you, thank you, thank you. Now, please tell me what to do with them.

> In Psalm 23:4, David stands assured of God's "with-ness": "I will fear no evil, for you are with me." So ladies, how do we get from here to there? How do we come to know, like David did, how to live out on Earth what we have become in Heaven?

It is one thing to say, "God is with me," and yet a whole other thing to live a life like we believe it. So often, like the day I was married, we take the vow and have no idea how to *be* what we have become.

"Lord, we want to walk through this world not only proclaiming Your Presence, but also living lives that look like we *believe* that You are with us. Please help us, Jesus, walk with You even through the valley of the shadow of death and not fear. Help us to be what, by Your grace, we have become. Amen."

In Matthew 1:18-23, we catch a glimpse of the beginning of Christ's earthly story.

Let's go there together. Read these verses and answer the following question.

> There are two names mentioned here. What are they and what do they mean based on what is stated in the Scriptures?

Immanuel, the *with* of God. Perhaps no other name given for Jesus brings me such comfort as this one. I love how the Message speaks of Christ's coming in John 1:14, "The WORD became flesh and blood, and moved into the neighborhood." Despite us, He comes to live with us and know us. He moves into our homes, He invades our lives and hearts, until, through the miracle of His grace, He has become one with us. He descends on our world, hoping that we might choose to ascend to His. He entrusts Himself to us, in hopes that we might entrusts ourselves to Him. The words of 1 John 4:19 take on new depth as we come to understand the truth that, "We love because he first loved us."

How do you respond to knowing that Christ has entrusted Himself to you?

We sheep are so self-driven that we can often make even knowing our Shepherd about us. We create a performance-based relationship with Him instead of a real relationship with Him. We think, "If we are good little lambs, He will be good to us. But if we are bad little lambs, we deserve what we get." We often unknowingly subject God to *our* rules and expect Him to perform based on *our* standards. When we do this, we miss the whole point of who He is and why He came. We see it as a give and take relationship because that is what we would expect from man. We do not realize that we have absolutely nothing to give.

Often like the church at Laodicea in Revelation 3, we do not realize the true depravity of our nature.

Please read, Revelation 3:15-18, and answer the following questions.

In verse 16, Christ says that He will do what to those who are "lukewarm?"

In verse 17, He states the attitude of those who have become lukewarm. Do you recognize any of these attitudes in yourself? If so, what are they?

It is easy to think that we have a proper perspective of who God is and how much we need Him, but our actions never lie. Each day we venture out into the world without a clear and distinct awareness of our own depravity and need for God. We are behaving just as this church did: lukewarm.

In verse 18, Christ directly states what it is we need from Him and what He came to give us. Please write below what those are that are listed.

There are three things He uses to represent the needs of each human: gold, our need for security and provision; white garments, our need to live shame free lives, to live free from the ravages of sin; and salve for our eyes so that we might be able to truly see what is important in this world, what is eternal.

Out of these three provisions, which one do you feel you are most in need of?

For me, it is the white garments. Each day, I struggle with my fleshly desire to hide from the world. I know what I am and it terrifies me. Yet, each day Immanuel, Christ's own *with*, is there to greet me and remind me that I have no need to hide anymore. He places His own robe across my shoulders and I am able to be what, by His grace, He has allowed me to become. I am His, and each day I acknowledge that, I am free to live out *true life* in this world. In Him, it is never a give and take relationship. It is take and take and take until all that we are is covered by all that He is.

Sweet sister, just as my husband made the decision to enter in to our little, broken family and become one with us, so too has Christ entered into your broken body and decided to become one with you. He has moved His furniture into your heart with plans to stay. Open your eyes! He is not in Heaven, far above you, looking down over you to judge your every move. He is in your heart right now, at this very moment, and has made and is making all things new inside of you. He is your own personal "with," and He is God.

Take a moment right here and ponder that miracle. Think of everything wonderful and grand about God, the very One who created the universe and all that is in it, the One who descended on the mountain of God in a cloud of fire and smoke, and the One who can part waters, make dead men come to life, and create anything out of nothing at all. *He* is inside of you right now. Reflect on that below. Can you believe it or does it still seem far away? Please be honest below in responding to this.

I love to read the accounts of Christ's birth. It is still hard for me to believe and comprehend that God became small enough to fit into the tiny body of a newborn baby. We will close our study today by looking in to this event, the day God moved in to our skin to become one of us.

Please join me in reading Luke 2:6-7 and then 8-14.

Who were the very first to hear of this miracle birth?

Back during the time of Christ's birth, the Israelites considered shepherds a despised class because their work kept them from keeping ceremonial law. They were the lowest of the low; they were not even allowed to give evidence in the courts. I find it so thrilling that these are the ones that God decided to share His greatest news with.

"Fear not, for behold, I bring you good news of great joy that will be for all the people. For unto you is born this day in the city of David, a Savior, who is Christ the Lord. And this will be a sign for you; you will find a baby wrapped in swaddling cloths and lying in a manger." And suddenly there was with the angel a multitude of the heavenly hosts praising God and saying, 'Glory to God in the highest, and on earth, peace among those with whom he is pleased!" Luke 2:10-14

"For in him all the fullness of God was pleased to dwell, and through him to reconcile to himself all things, whether on earth or in heaven, making peace through the blood of his cross." Colossians 1:19-20

Here is poem, my rendition of what that first "Holy Night" may have been like, I pray that it helps you draw closer to heart of Christ, our Immanuel.

A Shepherds Night Before Christmas

'Twas the first night of Christmas
And all through the earth
All the heavens proclaimed
The miracle birth

Barren souls were all hunkered
Down warm in their beds
Unaware of angels' voices
Singing over their heads

Except for myself
And a few fellow men
And our flocks of sheep grazing
Quietly until then …

When suddenly heavenly light
Lit up the skies
My mind too small to grasp
What I saw with my eyes

An angel proclaiming
My own Savior's birth
Awakening in me
My own need for worth

"Why me?" I thought
As a new sight appeared
Thousands of angels proclaiming
"Your Messiah is Here!"

I thought my heart would jump
Right out of my chest
"Why me?" my mind raced
"I am unworthy to be blessed"

Then all of the sudden
It all disappeared
Leaving only their message
Ringing out in my ear

"Tonight in a manger,
Your Savior is born"
Holy God came from heaven,
Our flesh to adorn"

My heart pound with wonder
As in abandon I raced
Towards the star that shined down
On a most humble place

Tears flooded my eyes
As the foretold sight appeared
And at once my awe was suddenly
Replaced by earthly fear

"I am only a shepherd,
Not a man of great worth
Who am I to witness,
God's miracle birth?"

But the Lord seemed to answer
With His soft, still, small voice,
"To behold My Son or not,
It is only your choice"

"This Gift I present
To all men on earth
A chance to exchange
Your sin for new birth"

"But this choice must be yours
To choose Life or death
To stand on earth firmly
Or take in Heaven's Own Breath"

My feet started walking
Disobeying my doubt
And I thought, "This must be
What walking by faith is about"

Heaven's Light bathed my skin
And my dusty tears fell to earth's floor
As I presented myself
To my King to adore

"No man of great worth,
Only my presence I bring,
And my worship to give
To my now, new, known King"

And a voice spoke from heaven
But it came from within,
"You, My dear shepherd,
Are most worthy of men"

"In humility you came,
To behold My Son,
Who will shepherd My people
And make Us all One"

"I hammered a bridge
For all men to cross
My Own Presence I give
To all who are lost"

"Oh Holy Night …
When Christmas was born
When incarnate Flesh
Came to one day be torn"

"Oh Shepherd, my Lord,
My Truth, and my King
Happy birthday sweet Jesus
Your praises, I will sing"

Then I turned to make
My way back on home
Away from the Star
That had so brightly shone

And in joyous wonder
As I turned back towards earth
By some mystery I knew,
There had been more than one birth

My path filled with darkness
My soul filled with Light
A miracle surely took place
On that most Holy Night

No longer only a shepherd
But now God's own son
My new life eternal
Had somehow begun

So I wish you the same
On this most Holy Night
That your eyes will behold
His most precious Light

That His miracle birth
Will take place in you
And that your greatest gift this Christmas
Will be that of Life anew

Tis the night before Christmas
And all through the earth
May all men receive the gift
Of God's Love through Christ's birth!

God's first visitors on Earth were the outcasts, the unwanted, and the rejected. I love that He chose these to be his first to present himself to. They represent all of us who, whether we are willing to admit it or not, struggle with the brokenness that comes with being human. And yet, He is pleased with us; He wants us, and wants to make us well. The question is, do we want Him? Are we willing to let Him place the salve on our eyes so that we might see the reality of who has moved in to our hearts and lives?

"And she gave birth to her firstborn son and wrapped him in swaddling cloths and laid him in a manger, because there was no place for them in the inn." Luke 2:6

God's own Son came to be born in a town completely occupied in a physical sense, yet completely barren of life in a greater sense. Man's eyes were closed to what all Heaven was celebrating. What man could not yet see or appreciate, every star, angel, and heavenly being was caught up in the weight of the glory that had just become wrapped up in tiny human flesh: God's precious gift to all mankind. The "with of God" had come to Earth, only Earth did not know it. Sweet lamb, do not miss the opportunity to know who it is that came for you. Do not let the places in your heart stay occupied with your own perceptions of who He is. Make room for the reality of Him in your heart. It's okay if you don't know where to go from this point forward, if all you can say is, "Thank you, thank you, thank you. Now, please tell me what to do with Him." His "with" will lead you and guide you and, despite yourself, He will cause you to be what you have become.

> Please close by writing your own prayer below expressing your desire to experience His "with." You are so precious, thank you for being Ewe!

Day 4

The Valley of the Shadow of Death

<table>
<tr>
<td>

DAILY GRAIN

</td>
<td>

Please begin by prayerfully receiving God's Word to you through these Scriptures:

"...Your rod and your staff, they comfort me." Psalm 23:4(c)

"And have you forgotten the exhortation that addresses you as sons? 'My son, do not regard lightly the discipline of the Lord, nor be weary when reproved by him. For the Lord disciplines the one he loves, and chastises every son whom he receives." Hebrews 12:5-6

</td>
</tr>
</table>

One of my favorite movies of all time is *Seabiscuit*. It is based on a true story about a race horse that was written off; however, upon coming to belong to just the right mix of people who believed in him and loved him, he became one of the world's most legendary race horses. Early in Seabiscuit's life, he had been used to help in training other horses to win. The riders would tear into him with a crop (a small leather whip) to get him in line with the horse being trained, and then once they came neck to neck, his rider would pull his reigns back so that Seabiscuit would be forced to lose the race, therefore encouraging the other horse to win. This horse had the heart of a champion, yet his spirit had been crushed. The rod was continually used to keep him from what he knew at the time was his destiny. Seabiscuit became angry and uncontrollable. Had his new owners not bought him, he would have been destroyed. The rod had been used in his life in a way that abused and discouraged him. It is ironic how so often the tool meant to encourage us in the right direction can become the tool that destroys us. How blessed we are to have a good Shepherd who knows just how to use the rod in our lives to call us to live legendary lives.

What does Proverbs 13:24 and Proverbs 23:13-24 say about the rod?

The rod is a tool of discipline, and just as God instructs earthly fathers to act as disciplinarians in their homes, so He, as our Father, acts as our disciplinarian in our lives. We associate the need for disciplinary action with childhood, however, in God's kingdom we are always His children. Once we are His, we can never grow too old for a spanking.

What about you? In your walk with God so far, have you ever felt His rod of discipline in your life? How? Please share below.

What does Hebrews 12:3-13 say about our Father's rod of discipline and how it is used in our lives?

Have you, like Seabiscuit, had a rod used in your life that was used for harm, instead of for good?

If so, I am so sorry. This world has a way of perverting all that is good and using it for evil. As one who has experienced the same, I can tell you that there is no safer place to be than in the arms of a Father who loves you and who wants nothing more than to lead you to an abundant life. You don't have to be afraid of Him, for His heart is for you.

If you are like me and did not grow up with a father in your home, maybe these verses bring comfort to your heart as they do mine. There is something about knowing that a father cared enough to "not spare the rod" that always brought a sense of comfort and security to my heart. Although I did not have an earthly father to protect me in that way, my heart rejoices in the knowledge that my heavenly Father is still parenting me. He not only wants me to succeed here on Earth, but can see 1,000 years from now and knows how my time here will affect my not only my future on Earth, but also in Heaven. He knows what it will take for me, however hard, to live a life that is worthy of eternal reward. He knows that I am like a sheep who cannot always see beyond the next bite of grass, so He leads me into a life that will not only change Earth, but will change Heaven by my actions. Like a master chef, He knows just the right ingredients we need to become an unforgettable delight to Heaven.

How do you feel about knowing that our Father in Heaven must discipline us?

In ancient times and even today in places where sheep herding is still practiced as it once was, the shepherd's rod was his instrument of attack and defense. It was usually a short, heavy, wooden stick that was carefully chosen to fit the shepherd's hand. Even as a young boy, he would practice using his rod to fight off imagined attackers such as bears or lions. Often young shepherd boys competed to see how fast or far they could to hit a small object from a great distance with his rod. He would use it to protect his flock, not only from predators, but oftentimes, from the sheep themselves if they wandered too close to a dangerous cliff or an area where known parasites or poisonous plants were near. A shepherd's rod was so much a part of him that was like an extension of his own hand. It was instinct for him to use it to fight off any enemy and to go before to secure safe pastures for his flock to graze.

It is hard for us to imagine needing such a device today for we do not live the lives of shepherds who face great danger as they lead their sheep up and down mountainous terrain with potential danger lurking around every corner. Well, as I think about it, maybe we can relate to these guys (and gals) a little more than I thought. As a mother, or even just as a helper and influencer in the lives of others, I often feel like I am called to lead my "flock" in what seems like very dangerous terrain. The threats of divorce, depression, harmful influences, peer pressure, immorality, jealousy and bitterness are just a few of the dangers that I must try and steer my little flock away from when I am called upon the help them negotiate this rugged terrain called life.

What about you? Do you feel that God has given you a "flock" to lead in your life?

What are some of the potential dangers that you experience as you seek to lead others through life?

Matthew 7:13-24 directs us to, "Enter by the narrow gate. For the gate is wide and the way is easy that leads to destruction, and those who enter by it are many. For the gate is narrow and the way hard that leads to life, and those who find it are few."

Sisters, it is easy for us to sit in the same pasture and never experience the dangers and the adventures of life. However, in doing so, we are not only keeping life from ourselves, but also from those who we are called to lead and influence. What if you are the one shepherd that God created to lead a certain group of sheep? How do we do it? What is our rod? How can we, who are in such need of discipline ourselves, held others find their way?

Just as shepherds had a weapon to shield not only themselves, but also their sheep from the dangers of their constant mountainous journeys, so too have we been given a rod.

What does Ephesians 6:10-20 say about how we are to stand in this battle of Life?

Specifically, what does 6:17 say our "sword" is?

His Word is our only offensive weapon to stand against the enemy, and yet it is the only one we need.

As Seabiscuit came to know and trust his owner and his rider, he became an inspiration to the whole world during a time when the whole world needed inspiration, the Great Depression. One of my very favorite parts is when his rider, Red, who had been injured and was not going to be able to ride Seabiscuit in one of his biggest races, is explaining to the jockey who will be taking his place about how to deal with Seabiscuit during the race. He has the door closed so that he can express the secret of this amazing horse's ability to outrun any competitor (despite the fact that he was almost a whole foot shorter and much smaller than most other race horses). He explains to this rider that during the last leg of the race, he is to let Seabiscuit come eye to eye with the horse that is in the lead at that time, show him the crop (the instrument that had formerly been used to abuse him) and then let him go. He explains that the secret to Seabiscuit's ability is in his heart. Under the loving care of this amazing horse's rider and owner, the very instrument that had been, at one time, used to abuse him and kill his spirit, had now become the very tool that was used to catapult him into certain victory every time he entered a racetrack. It was almost as if each time Seabiscuit was in that old familiar place again, eye to eye with his competitor, and then shown that rod that had been used to hold him back at one time, a flip switched in his heart and he was able to experience a freedom that he had never been given before: the freedom to experience victory. Sweet sister, our Father does the same for us. The very areas of our lives that we have experienced the most defeat in, when given the chance to be nourished and grown through His rod of discipline, will become the very areas of our lives that will cause us to live the victory of a legendary life.

"Therefore, since we are surrounded by so great a cloud of witnesses, let us also lay aside every weight, and sin which clings so closely, and let us run with endurance the race that is set before us, looking to Jesus, the founder and perfecter of our faith, who for the joy that was set before him, endured the cross, despising the shame, and seated at the right hand of the throne of God." Hebrews 12:1-2

Whether you know it or not sister, you are in the race of your life, and there is an audience not only on Earth, but also in Heaven who are cheering you on. The victory does not depend on circumstances or individual gifting, it depends on your heart. Let God do whatever it takes to catapult you into victory. Only he knows the recipe it will take to give you a victorious heart.

Please close in a prayer of gratitude for our Shepherd's rod that is used to bring us towards victory in Christ.

Day 5

The Valley of the Shadow of Death

DAILY GRAIN	Please begin by prayerfully receiving God's Word to you through these Scriptures: *"...Your rod and your staff, they comfort me." Psalm 23:4(c)* *"Whenever Moses held up his hand, Israel prevailed, and whenever he lowered his hand, Amalek prevailed." Exodus 17:11* *"And over his head they put the charge against him, which read, "This is Jesus, the King of the Jews." Matthew 27:37*

Our laughter was the only sound louder than the crashing waves all around us. My brothers and I were feeling more brave as we moved from jumping over the waves in the shallower waters of the beach to letting the waves carry us as we ventured further and further in to the ocean. One last glance to our mom camped out on shore gave me all the confidence I needed to rise to the challenge of this new adventure. Before long, I was lost in my own bliss as the crashing waves became smooth rollers that carried my feet right out from underneath me. It was just dangerous enough to be thrilling, however it was not long before the "what ifs" of the deep overwhelmed my sense of playful adventure. In an instant I noticed that the sound of my brothers' voices had drifted off. Nearing panic, I peered all around me in search for my mom or the sight of anything familiar. There was none. I had drifted somewhere far away and the once playful current of the deep became my antagonist as I began to push my way against the current in search of anything familiar.

Just as the ocean can carry us off without our even realizing it, there is a current in this world. It is so familiar to us that few of us even notice the subtleties of its presence until we are caught in its undertow and drowning in the murky darkness of its waters. It is the current of sin and death that man came to exist in at the very beginning. Just like Eve, we buy into its appearance (see Genesis 3). How can something that looks so good be bad? So, we bite into it and allow its current to carry us away not realizing that we are sinking deeper and deeper into its grip. The words of Proverbs 4:19 describe this well, "The way of the wicked is like deep darkness; they do not know over what they stumble," and Proverbs 14:12 which says, "There is a way that seems right to a man, but it's end is the way to death."

> Have you ever felt as if you were being carried away by the currents of this world? If so, in what ways? Please describe your experience below.

There are some of us who, by God's grace, come to that place where we are able to recognize our need for someone on shore to rescue us from the deep. Like a lifeguard tossing out his crook, Christ throws to us His own life and pulls us to the surface again. With new eyes we are able to *see* the reality of our danger and the miracle of our Shepherd and Savior. He smiles at us and laughs with us as He teaches us not only how to walk through the current victoriously, but also how to walk on water. The very current that once threatened our lives becomes the pavement under our feet as we learn to follow our good Shepherd.

Both in Hebrew and Greek, the word "staff" indicates not only a shepherd's staff to be used in the care and transportation of sheep, but also an emblem of authority or power. The word for scepter is often interchanged with the word staff. A king's scepter was a tangible representation of his power and authority to judge and rule his people. I find it interesting how often God uses the task of shepherding sheep to prepare his future leaders for the greater responsibility of shepherding his people. Jacob and all of his sons (representing the 12 tribes of Israel), Moses, and David were all shepherds before God called them to greater purposes.

Today we will spend time observing the day one shepherd began his transition from lowly shepherd to servant leader of God's people, Israel.

Please turn with me to 1 Samuel 17:1-50 and read the story of David and then answer the questions below.

For what purpose was David sent to the battlefield?

What was the condition of the Israel army when David arrived (were they winning the fight or losing)?

What does David ask in verse 26?

What was David's brother's response in verse 28?

Do you ever experience other's anger when you attempt to move forward with God? If so, please share what you believe to be the reasons below.

Verses 36-46 speak vividly about David's confidence level. What are some of his actions that display his confidence? Who or what does his confidence seem to be in?

Verse 47 sums up one of David's greatest testaments of faith and one that seemed to carry him all through his life. Who and how does David say that battles are won?

In the same verse, whose hands does David say that Goliath will be given into?

His or all of Israel's?

A young shepherd boy with the courage of a lion inspires a whole army to stand and fight for the victory that the Lord has already guaranteed. We so often think that it is our gifts, talents, money or power that allow some to *rule* in life while others stand by and watch. However, we see through David's courage that it is not those things at all that cause one to rule or lead. It is faith in God, a knowledge and trust in the victory that has already been won that causes some to stand out and lead us all. So often we believe that it is all up to us to fight for victory, but in Christ we are never called to fight for the victory, we are called to stand in the One who has already secured our victory. We have every right to be afraid when we think we are the ones who are called to fight because, in ourselves, we have no possibility of winning. The current is way too strong for us to begin to swim against. However, Christ came to give us the victory so that we never have to fight a battle we can't win. We simply stand in the victory of the battle that was already won.

Have you ever become fearful or afraid at the thought of having to fight a spiritual battle?

Moses paints a perfect picture of how we win our battles in Exodus 17:8-16. Let's go there now and catch a glimpse.

After reading Exodus 17:8-16, answer the following questions.

What was in Moses hand?

What happened whenever Moses became weary and his hands drooped?

How did Moses keep his hands up?

What was the name of the altar that Moses built?

"The LORD is my banner," I cannot think of any better covering! My daughter, Faith, has a strong battle with fear. Each night as she goes to bed, she prays, "Lord, tuck me under Your wing to keep me safe." Like us and like Israel, she needs to be reminded that her Shepherd not only is for her, but that He is literally standing up over her, protecting her with His own life. He is our banner, and that banner over us is love.

In verse 16, Moses says something that seems a little strange. "A hand upon the throne of the LORD! The LORD will have war with Amalek from generation to generation."

In ancient days, no one could approach a king unless he had held out his scepter for the person to touch. For one to "touch the king's scepter" was to be welcomed and protected by the king himself. Sweet One, we have been given the forever welcome of a held-out scepter from the King of Kings and Lord of Lords. When, by faith, we reach out to Him, we are touching the very throne of Heaven. He will be at war with all that keeps us from knowing and believing all that He is to us for generation to generation.

In Genesis 49:10, Jacob (Israel) is giving his blessings to his sons (the 12 tribes of Israel). When he comes to Judah he says, "The scepter shall not depart from Judah, nor the ruler's staff from between his feet ..." I love that, in his wisdom and grace, God has Jacob use both words, "scepter and staff," to depict the lineage of our Christ (the Lion of the tribe of Judah.) He is both our good Shepherd and our powerful

King. My heart grows tender at the impact of the words, "between His feet." Matthew 27:37 reminds us of the day that our Shepherd King also became our sacrificial lamb, "And over his head they put the charge against him, which read, 'This is Jesus, the King of the Jews.'" Roman criminal procedure demanded that a certificate of crime be attached to each person convicted of a crime in a Roman court, especially in the case of a criminal being executed. The charge given to Jesus was treason. A sign mockingly placed above his head proclaimed to the world the crime that Jesus was to die for, He claimed to be a king. No scepter in His hand, only a sign hung "between His feet," proclaiming his royalty to the world to whom He died for, a loyal King laying down His scepter in exchange for a cross. A charge given and hung between two nail pierced feet as He exchanged His scepter for a cross that would ensure each of us the chance to become rulers in His own kingdom. No one there, except for God to witness the moment that each of our sins became His sentence and all of His royalty became our possibility.

I find Christ's charge ironic. Treason is defined as a violation of allegiance toward one's country or sovereign, especially the betrayal of one's country by waging war against it or by consciously and purposely acting to aid its **enemies**. Romans 5:10 states, "For if while we were **enemies** we were reconciled to God by the death of his Son, much more, now that we are reconciled, shall we be saved by his life." Something about this really hits home with me, for I know how often my allegiance to Christ any given moment is challenged. My mind has such a desire for autonomy, yet my heart wants to fully belong to Christ. Knowing that what Christ did on the cross has paid for every time my mind wins out over my heart makes me feel so secure in Him. He knew that I would be guilty of treason against Him, yet still chose to take my place. What a Savior, and what a King!

> What about you? How do you respond to your own charge of treason? Does this change, in any way, your feelings about what Christ did for you on the cross?

We will close by taking a final look at our Shepherd King, only this time, He is not in the pasture with us. Meet me in Revelation 4:1-11 and let's read it together as we ponder the wonder and awe of God's throne in Heaven.

> After reading that description, which aspect of this vision stands out to you the most and why?

Now, my favorite part, let's read Revelation 3:19-21, what do these verses say will be given to "the one who overcomes?"

My eyes fill with tears each time I ponder our Savior's unselfish desire to share His glory with us who are just sheep. When I look at myself, I do not see royalty or anything worthy of Heaven, but when He looks at us, He sees His pearl of great price, His greatest treasure, the one He cannot wait to share His throne with.

Sweet sister, let's commit to doing whatever it takes to hold up our staff to stay under the banner of the victory that He has given us. The Enemy wants to sweep us away through the current that exists in our ignorance of our value to Christ. Do not give in; when you become weary, find friends to help you hold up God's staff of victory. Hold up your hand, Sweet One, you were not created to sink under this world's water, but to walk on it! Get up and remember who you are, a conquer through Christ!

Please close in a prayer thanking your Shepherd for His victory.

Week 3

The LORD Is My Shepherd; I Shall Not Want

Fill in the blanks below with the words according to the lesson
sacrifice, disobedience, need, vine, resting, life,

Hebrews 4:1 *"Therefore, while the promise of entering his rest still stands, let us fear lest any of you should seem to have failed to reach it."*

God sees not _____ in Him as _____.

Sometimes we don't think we _____ a Shepherd.

There is no _____ outside of the _____.

The very first mention of love had to do with _____.

Notes_____

_____

_____

_____

_____

_____

_____

_____

_____

Day 1

You Prepare A Table For Me

DAILY GRAIN	Please begin by prayerfully receiving God's Word to you through these Scriptures: *"You prepare a table before me in the presence of my enemies ..." Psalm 23:5(a)* *"... Your rod and your staff, they comfort me." Psalm 23:4(c)* *"Love is patient and kind; love does not envy or boast; it is not arrogant or rude. It does not insist on its own way; it is not irritable or resentful; it does not rejoice at wrongdoing, but rejoices with the truth. "Love bears all things, believes all things, hopes all things, endures all things. Love never ends ..." 1 Corinthians 13:4-8a*

I remember the moment so well, although I cannot remember what it was I was so angry with my husband about. It was one of those mornings where everything was wrong; I just could not seem to get it right with God, I knew that my heart was full of all the wrong intentions, yet I did not know what to do about it. So, after having a lengthy "tattle tale on my husband session" with the Lord where I went over all of my typical complaints making sure that God knew that I would stay in this marriage because I *have to* love this man who *He* made me marry. I put on my headphones and turned the music up really loud on my iPod in hopes of drowning out that voice inside my head that always seemed to be taunting me, "you are the problem, you are the problem!" I skipped over the Christian tunes, and I knew that I was not being very Christ-like at that moment and that I would eventually have to come back around, but for now I was mad! I had been treated wrongly and I deserved to feel what I was feeling, didn't I?

It was during the song *One* by U2 when I heard the unmistakable voice of my Shepherd. My shock over hearing God through a secular song overwhelmed my sense of righteous indignation as I screamed out, "God, I had no idea You could speak through U2, how cool are You!" I remember trying to get a mental image of Jesus up there in Heaven jamming out to U2 and it just cracked me up. My whole mood changed in an instant; it is amazing how our Shepherd's voice can do that. At the sound of His call, we forget all about our own pasture and are ready to follow wherever He is leading. It was when Bono pelted out the lyrics, "one love, one life, you *get* to share it …" that I got the point that Christ was making clear to my heart that morning. "Rhonda, you don't ever *have* to love anyone, you *get* to!" I sat down amidst the huge pile of laundry I had been working on and let those words sink in. "I get to love, I *get* to … love … I *get* to LOVE!"

I wanted to save our last and most obvious lesson about the "staff" of our Shepherd until we came to this portion of Psalm 23; the portion that deals with how our Shepherd leads us to deal with our enemies. According to Phillip Keller's *A Shepherd Looks at Psalm 23*, "The staff, more than any other item of his personal equipment, identifies the shepherd as a shepherd. No one in any other profession carries a shepherd's staff." (pp. 97-98, Keller). A shepherd specially creates each staff for his specific flock. The staff symbolizes the shepherd's desire to look after not only his flock's safety, but also his desire to comfort his flock. The staff consists of a long, slender piece of wood with a crook or hook on its end. It is used to guide sheep, to lift them up when they fall, and to draw them not only close to each other, but also close to their shepherd. In our Christian walk, the Holy Spirit most resembles our Shepherd's staff. He is our guide and our comfort. He lifts us when we fall, and He leads us towards love, always, whether it is towards loving one another or towards loving Christ. Jesus tells us in John 16:13, "When the Spirit of truth comes, he will guide you into all truth, for he will not speak of his own authority, but whatever he hears he will speak, and he will declare to you the things that are to come." Like the slender, wooden staff pressing against the sheep's side, directing it, so our Shepherd uses His Spirit to press up against our soul and lead us towards the narrow path that is leading to life.

So how do we know what determines the direction our Shepherd is leading? John 17 gives us a clear view of our ultimate destination during our earthly stay. Let's go there together and see if we can catch a glimpse of our destiny.

Please meet me in John 17:1-26 and after reading Christ's High Priestly prayer, answer the following questions.

What does Christ say eternal life is (verse 3)?

Whom is Christ praying for (verse 9)?

In what way are those whom He is praying for part of the world (verse 9-11&15)?

In verse 17, Christ asks the Father to do what?

What is significant about verse 20?

What word is mentioned 4 times in verses 21-23? Why do you feel that this word is so significant to Christ that He would mention it so many times?

What does Christ say in verse 26 that He will continue to make known to us?

This High Priest's duty was to represent the whole people. In Christ's time, he would have been the one who was consecrated (set apart through purification) to present the sin offering to the Lord on behalf of the people (the Israelites). Christ said this prayer shortly before He went to the cross. This prayer represents a type of summary of Christ's purpose for coming to earth; " …that they might become perfectly one, so that the world may know that [God] sent me and loved them even as [God] loved me." John 17:23.

When I read this prayer, I am reminded that there is a greater purpose for why I am here. Like a passenger on a journey who gets distracted by all the places to stop on the way, I easily forget that I have a destination, that I was created to go somewhere. In this prayer, Christ lays it all out: we are here to become one with Him so that through that love we can become one with each another. If we ever wonder why the world does not know about Christ and why they think that Christians are such hypocrites, it is because we do not live in this way. We make our journey about the next pit stop instead of about our destination. Christ mentions in this prayer two ways the whole world will know that He is who He says He is and that we are who He says we are: when we believe in Him through His word and are one with each other and with Him and also when we receive the glory that He gave us so that we might be perfectly one just as He and the Father are one. So often I wonder how we can try to convince the world of something that we don't even seem to be convinced of ourselves. I must admit that I don't wake up every morning knowing that I have God's glory in me and ready to believe everything that He says in His word is true towards me. However, I do admit that I want to do those things, to be convinced so strongly of Christ's provision for me.

How are you doing with your awareness of all that you are in Christ?

I am comforted by my knowledge that Christ does not expect us to do things that alone we have no ability to fulfill. He gave us a Shepherd, His own Spirit to lead us and guide us into becoming all that we were created to be. The words of Christ in John 14:26 are such a comfort to me: "But the Helper, the Holy Spirit, whom the Father will send in my name, he will teach you all things and bring to your remembrance all that I have said to you." So, at any given moment, in any given circumstance, I have a Helper there to help me choose the way that leads to my destination. Like a shepherd, He places his staff against my side and directs me forward, moving me away from what is temporary and toward what is eternal.

Still, there are so many questions and so many ways that I begin to try and argue out what that way is. That is where Bono comes back in to the picture: "One love, one life, you *get* to share it." The one way we can always know it is Christ who is leading us is that He will always lead us to love. 1 John 4:7 says, "Beloved, let us love one another, for love is from God, and whoever loves has been born of God and knows God." Over and over in the Scriptures we are told that *love* is the primary indicator of God's presence. But what is love? How do we recognize it? As a woman, how can I determine what love is over lust, feelings, or hormones? The word love has taken on a multitude of meanings and expressions. Trying to pick out the real things in this world can sometimes be like trying to pick out which chocolate bar is healthiest for us; our judgment is very colored by what we want to see. However, we are blessed that in Scripture God has given us both a microscope and a telescope to catch a glimpse of both the breadth and the intricacy of love.

> Let's head over to 1 Corinthians 13:4-13 and read the love chapter together. Feel free to record any thoughts or challenges that stand out to you below.

1 John 4:16(b) reminds us, "God is love, and whoever abides in love abides in God, and God abides in him." After reading this verse, go back and read 1 Corinthians 13:4-8 again, only this time substitute Christ's name each time you see the word love.

> How did that exercise impact your understanding of those verses? Please share below.

Now, according to 1 John 4:16 (written above), when we abide in love, we are abiding in God. With this in mind, I want you to go back and read 1 Corinthians 13:4-8 again, but this time place your name each time you see the word love.

> Wow, that really impacts me as I am reminded once again who I am called to be while living here on Earth. Out of all the characteristics named in those verses, which one did you find the most challenging?

It may a good idea to place your name with that part of the Scripture on a card in a place where you can see it often as a way to remind yourself that you have the power through Christ is overcome all of your *self* that keeps you from exhibiting Christ's character. For me, it is, "Rhonda does not insist on her own way; is not irritable or resentful." It is so easy for me to *feel* those things and therefore respond to them as if they are true. It is hard for me to remind myself that I have the power through Christ to *choose* to be different than how I feel. My faithful Shepherd is there each moment with me, reaching out His staff to direct me towards love each time. If I can quiet the noise and just take a second to listen, I can hear Him reminding me, "One love, one life, you *get* to share it." I am reminded of my greater calling, that because I know Christ, I *get* to love people instead of responding to how they might make me feel. He gives me more than enough love to give away. He is my love.

If we can just *get to* love, He will give us all we need to give away.

Please close in a prayer today, ladies, thanking Christ for the love that He lets us share with Him.

Don't Scatter and Scoot!

1 Peter 5:8 "Be sober-minded, be watchful. Your adversary the devil prowls around like a roaring lion, seeking someone to devour."

Genesis 4:6-7. "The LORD said to Cain, "Why are you angry, and why has your face fallen? If you do well, will you not be accepted? And if you do not do well, sin is crouching at your door. Its desire is for you, but you must rule over it."

Sheep are prey animals, and as such often use avoidance and rapid flight to avoid being eaten when predators draw near. I don't know about you, but I am VERY sheep-like in this way. We all have different "predators", ways that the enemy comes after us and tries to separate us from our herd so he can attack. I have seen this is my own family. When conflicts arise, it is so easy to want to turn against one another instead of banding together to realize who the *REAL* enemy is.

Ephesians 6:12 reminds us, "For we do not wrestle against flesh and blood, but against the rulers, against the authorities, against the cosmic power over this present darkness, against the spiritual forces of evil in the heavenly places."

Picture this image with me; maybe it's your home, your work, your church, or your school. There is a lion, hungry for prey, outside pacing around, intimidating everyone inside with unimaginable thoughts, worldly thoughts. These are things that you don't want to think about one another, but right at this moment your feelings are screaming louder than any other voice. All you want them to do is to get away from you, however you have no idea the unimaginable cost that sits crouching at the door, ready to engulf whoever it is that flees the flock.

Genesis 4:6-7. "The LORD said to Cain, "Why are you angry, and why has your face fallen? If you do well, will you not be accepted? And if you do not do well, sin is crouching at your door. Its desire is for you, but you must rule over it."

Like me, have you experienced a time when you have been tempted to *scoot and scatter?* Ask Jesus to show you the truth about this pattern in your life and to help shepherd you in HIS way.

Domesticated sheep have learned to do two things when a predator draws near; they herd together with ears perked up, and they draw near to their shepherd.

Day 2

You Prepare A Table For Me

DAILY GRAIN	Please begin by prayerfully receiving God's Word to you through these Scriptures: *"You prepare a table before me in the presence of my enemies ..." Psalm 23:5(a)* *"And the angel of the LORD came again a second time and touched him and said, "Arise and eat, for the journey is too great for you." 1 Kings 19:7*

She will be three next month and as I ponder the past three years since her birth, my eyes brim with tears. Her survival alone has been one of God's greatest outward testimonies of His ability to carry His kids through anything. On a more personal note, her survival has secured knowledge in my own heart of the inner workings Christ has done in my life. This girl who was a runner, a quitter, and a coward is still there, still alive, breathing, and changing her own little corner of the world. Her name is Pink Armor and she was born in the heart of a woman that I did not even know existed a little over three years ago. I will never forget the day that I and two other women sat in an empty church room and talked about the dream that one woman had to create a Bible study class for women. I had no idea what was even going on until shortly before the meeting finished (yes, I am blond) when I asked, "now, what are we doing?" "We are starting a Bible study." That was when it all hit me. I was able to take a small peek behind the veil of what God has been doing in my own life for the prior few years when I knew that He was calling me to teach women the Bible. He is so wise to get me into that meeting before I knew exactly what was going on, so that I could not weasel my way out of what He had prepared me for. The reason why her survival is such a miracle to me is because of all that has happened to potentially destroy it. Each attack from the enemy on any one of us could have caused the fatal blow that secured the death of this miracle girl. It did not take long after the birth of this class before we began seeing the signs that the enemy was on to us. As our name implies, we had come to wage war on his turf, the hearts of women he wanted to destroy. We were coming to train and teach them to use Pink Armor; to be feminine warriors who could fight off his attempts to destroy them. As I look back now, I can see that she is alive today because Christ has taught each one of *us* how to use Pink Armor to fight off the enemies attempts to destroy not only us, but what we were trying to do for God's kingdom. It would take a whole book to tell you all of the ways the enemy has tried to take us down, but here are just a few: pregnancy (morning sickness), sickness (our own and that of our children), discouragement, dissentions, bitterness, marriage conflicts and struggles, premature babies, miscarriages, devastating diagnosis, financial struggles, personal struggles with sin, and at times hopelessness. This journey has definitely been too great for us, but we have been so blessed to have a Shepherd who takes us beyond ourselves, out to the open fields of life where He then spreads out a blanket and sets up a picnic for us to eat from. All of this happens while our enemies must stand around and watch, knowing that we are untouchable in His presence.

What about you? What are some of the struggles that you are facing right now?

Can you see where the enemy is trying to "take you down?"

Through much of the Bible, there seems to be this *objective* that God is trying to reach in our lives. It extends all the way back from Genesis, where He calls Abraham to leave Haran, to Revelation, where Christ is asking the church of Laodicea to stop being lukewarm and come in to a real relationship with Him. The objective seems to call us out of our measly, little worlds and in to the endless possibilities of His. "The thief comes only to steal and kill and destroy. I came that they may have **life** and have it abundantly" John 10:10 (emphasis mine). Long before any of us even knew how to walk, the thief was already laying out his groundwork to destroy us. Sometimes we think that this "destruction" is general in nature; we think our bad habits, destructive choices, and brushes with death and hate are only a consequence of living in a fallen world. Because we do not realize our unimaginable worth to our Shepherd and God, we have no idea of the threat we are to the enemy of our souls. Why would he have a plan for you? Who are you that he would even be worried about your life? As long as we continue to have thoughts like these, he has us just where he wants us. If he can just keep us focused on survival and not grasping what it truly is to *live*, he has us. Without many of us even knowing it, the thief has come and stolen our life out from underneath us. But Christ has come; His greatest gift to us is life abundant! So often we turn our walk with Christ into a relationship with a list of "do's" and "don'ts" instead of a real, living, breathing, loving and leading God. We forget that our Maker does not live in temples made with human hands (Acts 17:24), and we never stop to ponder whether our god is truly God or just some conjured up self-made *idea* of who God is. Oswald Chambers said, "Every time you venture out in the life of faith, you will find something in your common-sense circumstances that flatly contradicts your faith." (My Utmost for His Highest, Aug. 29th) If we have made up a god who fits right in line with our "common sense," a safe god who never challenges our thoughts and actions, then we have bought into the perfect scheme of the enemy. He is leading us and guiding us with his own staff towards a place of death, and it is up to us to begin to recognize and follow our true Shepherd towards life.

> In your walk with God, can you recognize any ways you have limited Him?

> How do you describe faith? Do you feel that your walk with Him now is based on true faith?

This is so important because until we can *see* the path we are on, we won't know whom it is we have been following. In Christ, there is no way to follow Him other than through faith. Satan's schemes can seem so alluring because his plans seem to include "sight." Like sheep whose only concern is the next munch of grass, we follow the breadcrumbs, not realizing that we are taking ourselves and all those behind us straight down his path to death and destruction. Walking with Christ seems so much harder because we must walk by faith, which by definition means to walk without sight. We must follow a Shepherd, which means that we must trust Him to lead us to a good place. It all boils down to one question: do you trust your Shepherd more than yourself?

> How are you doing at your faith journey? In what ways do you sometimes find it hard to trust your Shepherd over yourself?

I love how God provides for us, " …He remembers that we are dust …" (Psalm 103:14). He knows that real faith is hard for us to lay hold of, so He provided us with countless stories about men and women who struggled to have faith in Him and overcame. Every major player in the Bible can fit in to one of two categories: those who had faith in God and those who did not. Today we will look at one of those men and his own wrestling match with choosing whether to go forward with faith in God or to give up.

Please join Elijah and me in 1 Kings 19:1-18. After reading, please answer the questions below.

Why was Elijah running?

What does he ask God in verse 4 and what comment does he make about himself?

Been there girls? I know I have those days when I want to turn in my shield of faith and get this life over with. How precious that God extends His grace and His strength just when we need it.

In verse 5, what was Elijah doing?

Do you perceive any relationship between our "rest" and God's ability to "touch us?"

In verse 7, the angel touches him a second time and tells Elijah, "Arise and eat, for the journey is too great for you." So often, it is not until we realize the weight of those very words that we are able to stand again and start going forward. We often forget whose journey this is, and God graciously causes us to come to that place where we must lay it all down again.

What question does God ask Elijah two times in verses 9 and 13?

What do you feel is God's reason for asking that particular question?

"What are we doing here?" "What on earth are we here for?" "Whose life is this?" "Why am I here?" These questions are some of those that bounce around in our heads, especially as we seek to live a life for Christ. So often, like Elijah, we forget where we are, and we need God to remind us that we are in Him. We are so tempted to let the earthquakes, fires, and strong winds of life challenge our awareness of where we are. He reaches in to our hearts and reacquaints our hearts to His "still, small voice" that reminds us where our true home is: in Him. I love that this account of Elijah takes place just after his greatest moments of glorifying God on Earth. Between 1 Kings 17:17-18:46, Elijah not only raises a boy from the dead, he confronts a king and all the prophets of Baal regarding who the true God is, has 450 prophets of Baal killed, gives news about a major drought ending, climbs a mountain and prays seven times, and then he runs down the mountain fast enough to outrun the king who was on horseback (all the while holding up his garments). It had been quite a time for Elijah and I imagine that he was exhausted. I find it interesting that we often have our greatest moments of doubt right after we have made huge strides with God. Perhaps we need to be reminded that we are still touchable, that we are still weak and weary sheep who still need their Shepherd.

When was the last time you had a time a great triumph with God that was followed by a great time of testing? Please share about it.

I have written in an old journal that I ran across yesterday, "sometimes God uses the lion to accomplish His work." I believe what God's Word says in James 1:13, "let no one say when he is being tempted, "I am being tempted by God," for God cannot be tempted with evil, and he himself tempts no one." However, just as some of us parents do when we want our kids to learn, He lets us have our way and deal with the consequences of our actions. As His Word says, "You prepare a table before me in the presence of my enemies …" (Psalm 23:5a). He sets the table with all of the bread of Heaven and living waters we need to nourish and hydrate ourselves in this "journey that is too great for us." Sisters, may we all be willing to done our pink armor and fight like girls to maintain trust for our Shepherd when the enemy tries to steal our hearts away from the table of abundant life that our Father and Shepherd has provided for us.

Please close in a prayer thanking Him for the table of life that He has set out for us.

Day 3

You Prepare A Table For Me

DAILY GRAIN	Please begin by prayerfully receiving God's Word to you through these Scriptures: *"You prepare a table before me in the presence of my enemies ..." Psalm 23:5(a)* *"And the Philistines seized him and gouged out his eyes and brought him down to Gaza and bound him with bronze shackles. And he ground at the mill in the prison." Judges 16:21*

My mom would kill me if she knew I was sharing this with you, I swore to never tell a soul right after it happened. We were on our way to San Antonio for a weekend get-away and were so excited for the chance to go have some fun, but also to get to catch up with each other. Now that I'm a mom, I seldom get the chance to keep my mom posted on all of the fascinating details of our family's lives. So we were knee deep in a conversation when nature called and we realized that it was time for a pit stop. We got back in the car to pick up our conversation where we had left off. It was almost two hours later when I asked, "Mom, didn't we already pass all of this?" We both gasped when we realized what we had done. After making our pit stop, I was turned around and went in the opposite direction from the way of our destination. We were so engrossed in our conversation that we failed to realize that we were headed back in the same direction we had left from. We made almost a complete circle and wasted four hours of our travel time going in the opposite direction. Did I mention that I am blond?

The Israelites spent forty years in the wilderness "going in the opposite direction," so it seemed. As we will see today, God often uses our turns in the wrong direction to help us discover some of the most telling aspects of who we truly are. Sometimes it takes us making another loop around the same bend we have seen over and over again for us to finally realize that we want to move on. In desperation, we finally turn our gaze from our trodden down path and notice a Shepherd waiting just outside the gate. How come we never noticed Him there before? Just as He always is, our Shepherd waits outside of our familiar paths, always challenging, always prodding us to new places in Himself. The words of Isaiah 48:6 come to mind, "You have heard; now see all this; and will you not declare it? From this time forth I announce to you new things, hidden things that you have not known." When we are following our Shepherd, we never have to worry about walking in circles; He is always leading us to "new things, hidden things that we have not known."

Speaking of circles, let's get to our main text for today as we learn a few lessons about circles from a man named Samson. We will pick up near the end of Samson's story. His story actually begins a few chapters back (in Judges 13 if you want to read up on him). Here is a brief low-down on Samson; he had been born during a time when Israel had fallen away from the Lord and had been taken into the hands of the Philistines. His mother had been unable to conceive, but an angel had given her word that she would have Samson and that she was to set him apart from birth through a Nazirite vow. This meant that he was to abstain from drinking alcohol, eating any unclean food, and that he was not to cut his hair. From the time of Samson's birth, the Lord blessed him with supernatural strength and power. God had set him apart to help the Israelites against the Philistines. Although Samson had these blessings, he had a shortcoming and weakness in the form of his lust for foreign women (with whom Israelites were forbidden to have relationships). After becoming a thorn in the Philistine's side due to his constant victory over them, he finally comes to the end of himself when he meets a woman named Delilah. This is where we will pick up Samson's story.

Please join me in Judges 16:4-31. After reading, please answer the questions below.

What does verse 4 say about how Samson felt towards Delilah?

Based on Delilah's actions toward Samson in the passage, what are her feelings towards Samson?

Why do you think Samson stayed in this relationship?

Verse 16 really spoke truth to me, "And when she pressed him hard with her words day after day, and urged him, his soul was vexed to death." The Lord badly wants to take us to new places, but the enemy badly wants to keep us going in circles, never experiencing God. Like a cart horse following the carrot tied to a string in front of its face, we follow the path that we think will bring us the fulfilment of our heart's desire, the next fix that our flesh needs. Only it is always out of reach. He "presses and urges us until we are vexed to death." Without even noticing, we have crossed the line from life to death. Like cattle entering the ramp that leads to the slaughter house or the drug addict who finally mixes that fatal concoction that he thinks will get him high again, we are trapped and don't realize it until it is too late.

In verse 20, what was Samson's response when he "woke from his sleep?"

What does it say about his awareness of losing the Lord's power?

So, at what point did God's power leave Samson?

The last strand of hair fell from Samson's head just as the last bit of God's anointing left him. The untouchable Samson would soon find out that it was God's touch that had saved him time and time again. However, Samson had become so lost in his own pursuits that he did not even notice the moment that God's glory left him. Like a neglected house that finally succumbs to the wear of time and elements, Samson's neglect for God's call on his life finally succumbed to the elements of Samson's selfish pursuits. Without even knowing it, God's glory had finally left him. Like a sheep skirting just outside the fence of the lavish, green pasture in search of what was beyond her reach, Samson spent his whole life seeking what was just outside of God's will for his life until God gave him what his actions had been leading up to his whole life: freedom from God's call.

In verse 21, what did the Philistine's do to Samson once they captured him?

A bald, bound, and blind Samson spent his days walking out literally the journey that his heart had always been on … a journey of circles. The mills of that day consisted of a wooden pin that was attached to two huge millstones. Slaves (or mules) would push a wooden pin attached to the upper stone in a circle over and over, grounding the grain underneath.

I love what verse 22 implies, "But the hair of his head began to grow again after it had been shaved." What do you think God was implying by this?

Little by little, just as Samson's hair was growing back, so was his heart growing softer and softer towards God. I imagine his tears flowing as he would think back over his life and all of the privilege that God had given him, and then how he had thrown it all away. I imagine him wrestling with his desire to ask God for another chance while, at the same time, knowing in his heart that he was not worthy to be heard. However, little by little, just as a sheep's wool grows, his hair was growing back. Each day as Samson grinded at that mill, his call was coming back. Whether we like it or not, God's plans for us cannot be thwarted. Just as Isaiah 14:24 says, "The LORD of hosts has sworn; As I have planned, so shall it be, as I have purposed, so shall it stand."

In verse 28, Samson calls out to the Lord. What does his willingness to call out to the Lord say about him?

What does verse 30 say about what Samson accomplished in his death?

Whether in our life or in or death, God's purpose is accomplished!

In the Bible, the wool of sheep represents our self, our *flesh* that must be removed for we *sheep* to experience the freedom from the weight of our thick covering, as well as from the parasites that have infested it. Just as a sheep's wool grows little by little each day and the sheep adjusts to the weight of it as it grows, so our hearts can become more and more calloused towards God without our even being aware of it. Just as the sheep meets its shearer in terror, not realizing that it will soon be free from the unimaginable weight of its wool, so we too must often meet our "Shearer." We are terrified at His coming, not realizing that we would soon have died under the weight of our "wool" had He not come to shave it from us. Samson was shaved both literally and spiritually, yet it took his "wool" coming off for God to make him touchable again.

What about you? Do you have any "wool" that needs to come off? Please explain below.

While your enemy watches, let Him shear you, Sweet One. Only He knows what it will take you free you from the heaviness of the wool that is weighing you down so that you don't have to walk in those circles any more. Let's be willing to leave our piles of wool right there next to our millstones and join the adventure of real life in Christ! Let's cause all of the plans of the enemy for us to come falling down on him as we let our Shepherd become our pillar of strength. Life was meant to be a race, but not one that is run on a track. Go, run, and see all that the Lord is laying out in abundant life for you. Aren't you tired of those old, familiar sights? Get out there girl, where the Shepherd is waiting to show you the "new things, hidden things that we have not known."

Please close in a prayer thanking our Shepherd for rescuing us from the constraining circles that the enemy has planned for us.

Day 4

You Prepare A Table For Me

DAILY GRAIN	Please begin by prayerfully receiving God's Word to you through these Scriptures: *"You prepare a table before me in the presence of my enemies …" Psalm 23:5(a)* *"I am not speaking of all of you; I know whom I have chosen. But the Scripture will be fulfilled, "He who ate my bread has lifted his heel against me." John 13:18*

I cannot remember when and how I first heard about John and Betty Stam, but will never forget their story and how it challenges me to trust God in all circumstances. It wasn't the way that they were brutally killed that challenges me, or the way that they were humiliated as they were paraded down the streets of the Chinese village of Tsingteh, China, where they had recently moved to become missionaries to this small, quaint village. It was the fact that they had a baby girl, Helen Priscilla, who had only recently been born. It was 1934 when this young, missionary family was attacked. Betty had just finished bathing her new daughter when a bandit horde of communists unexpectedly rushed on the small village. John and Betty were targeted as "enemies of the people" for their belief in Christ and their willingness to share Him with the surrounding villagers. As a mother, I cannot imagine anything worse than knowing that one of my children is in grave danger and there is nothing that I can do about it. As the couple was ordered to leave their home for the last time, Betty held her newborn daughter tucked snuggly in heavy winter blankets, perhaps hoping that the heaviness of the material might shield her from the horror of what was to come. John and Betty were thrown into a mud hut for the night where John was able to scribble a letter to the China Inland Mission Leaders. It read, "My wife, baby and myself are today in the hands of communist bandits. Whether we will be released or not no one knows. May God be magnified in our bodies whether by life or by death. Philippians 1:20." It was believed to have been early the next morning that John and Betty were taken out of the hut and murdered. Sometime during the night, Betty had tucked provisions, the letter, and a $10.00 bill inside of baby Helen's snuggle bunny, perhaps in hoping that, if found, someone might take her baby in and care for her. And that is exactly what happened the next day. Mr. Lo, who John had trained as a lay evangelist, risked his own life to follow the trail to where John and Betty had been taken as soon as he could. He snuck inside of the mud hut and, by chance, noticed the bundle of heavy winter blankets in the corner with baby Helen tucked inside. Miraculously, she had slept the entire 27 hours of the whole ordeal, never crying to give herself away — a silence that saved her life. She was later returned to her maternal grandparents who raised her until the age of five when her aunt adopted her and raised her as her own.

Stories like this one remind us that even the most faithful are not promised a safe or easy journey here on Earth. We might ask, how can God say that He, " …prepares a table before us in the presence of our enemies …"(Psalm 23:5(a) personalization mine), when He allows things like this to happen to those who are faithfully serving Him? There is truly no way to know all of the reasons that God allows what He chooses to allow. Just as He points out in Isaiah 55:8-9, "For my thoughts are not your thoughts, neither are your ways my ways, declares the LORD. For as the heavens are higher than the earth, so are my ways higher than your ways and my thoughts than your thoughts." However, we can hold on to the fact that He also promises that, " …for those who love God all things work together for good, for those who are called according to his purpose" (Romans 8:28). So we are left with a sort of wrestling match that happens in our hearts and minds when we see what looks like the enemy winning, but somehow God is causing all things to work for good? How can this be?

> What about you? Have you ever had an instant in your life where you question God's judgment of what He has allowed to go on?

> Have you ever experienced something that you thought was of "the enemy" working out for good? If so, how?

Could it be that we, who are merely human and are limited in our ability to "see," cannot fully comprehend what the word "good" entails in view of what God deems as "good?" Just as we only see the top of an iceberg whose immensity in size is concealed by the ocean, could it be that the totality of God's plan for "good" stays concealed beneath the ocean of His providence? How can we, who are limited, even conceive of what is really good and bad? Our perspectives stay colored by our own sheep-like tendency to want to stay away from pain and fear, while moving towards blessings and abundance. Only God can see the reality of what it will take to work our lives for good according to His purposes. Only He knows what to serve us on this table called life that will ensure we are full and ready for the "well done my good and faithful servant."

In John 13:1-35, we see one of Christ's last moments with His disciples. They are eating this meal together on the eve of the Passover, which is a day commemorating the day that God led the Israelites out of the captivity in Egypt. At this time, Christ's disciples have no idea that they are sitting with the Passover Lamb, and that the day of Passover will be the day that this Lamb will lead all of them (and us) out of captivity.

Please read John 13:1-35 and then answer the questions below.

According to verse 2, when did the enemy enter Judas' heart to betray Christ?

Verses 4-12 describe what Christ did during this meal. What did He do and who all took part in this act?

What do Christ's words in verse 10 imply about His knowledge of what was going to happen?

Did this knowledge keep Jesus from washing Judas' feet?

Have you ever experienced a circumstance in which, "he who has ate *your* bread has lifted his heel against *you*?" If so, please tell about it below.

Based on what Jesus says in verses 31-35, do Judas' actions play in to what God has planned to glorify Christ?

"You prepare a table before me in the presence of my enemies ..." Psalm 23:5(a). These words take on new depth as we realize that the table God may be setting is one in Heaven, not one here on Earth. When we think of these words, we see earthly justice served in ways that please fleshly desires. We cannot fathom that God has a bigger vision for us. In Heaven, a thousand years is but a day. God is using us right now, in these very moments to set our own table that we will dine from for all eternity. He loves us too much to allow our short sightedness to stand in the way of our eternal reward.

What do Revelation 19:6-9 say about a "feast?"

What does verse 8 say that we will be wearing?

One day, Beloved, we will sit across a table from John and Betty Stam and we will hear them tell us their side of the story, how in an instant all that was temporary gave way to all that was eternal. How Christ was holding them in His arms before their bodies ever hit the ground, how Betty's anxious thoughts about her daughter suddenly seemed ridiculous once she touched the hand of the One who is the beginning and the end of all. Tears may stream down their cheeks as they recall how their sacrifice spurred a great movement of young missionaries to surrender their lives to share the good news of Christ and how their martyrdom helped trigger a national reform movement in China that allowed many more missionaries to go to China and share Christ. Maybe they will recount the words of Paul, the last words that John wrote on Earth before he touched the face of Jesus, "For to me to live is Christ, and to die is gain." (Philippians 1:21). No matter what we have faced here on Earth or what we have yet in front of us, there will be no weeping at that time, only an immense gratitude for each and every stitch Christ used in our lives to knit an immaculate wedding gown — a wedding gown knit from our righteous deeds. Maybe He will even let us see it with the world as its backdrop and we will notice how brightly His righteousness shines in what is most un-right. And maybe then our hearts may grasp the magnitude of what we had in each moment spent here on Earth.

Precious one, our Shepherd knows where He is taking each one of us, not to give a happy and secure life on Earth, but to give us an eternal inheritance in Heaven. Don't let any enemy on this temporary Earth keep you from experiencing all that Christ has for you in eternity. Instead, let God use those who would harm you as landmarks to God's greater purposes. Just as Judas sat at God's table, let God use all of those He places at your table to shape and sharpen you for His eternal purposes.

Please close in a prayer for God's eternal vision for your life.

WEEK 4   BECOMING EWE

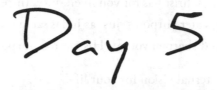

You Prepare A Table For Me

DAILY GRAIN 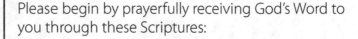	Please begin by prayerfully receiving God's Word to you through these Scriptures: *"…you anoint my head with oil; my cup overflows."* Psalm 23:5 (b) *"…And the LORD said, Rise, anoint him, for this is the one."* 1 Samuel 16:12(b)(NIV)

Kids just crack me up. I don't know if God uses any greater source in my life than my children to teach me the truth about myself and about Him. As I was contemplating how to introduce this portion of our lesson, I did not have but to look across the room as my four year old, Hope, gave me the perfect illustration. My older daughter, Faith, has had Noel, her cat, for over three years now. Noel knows exactly whom she belongs to. I will never understand how a cat that has been subjected to that much humiliation, teasing, and outright cat torture by one little girl can still love her so much. She waits till Faith is sleeping and curls up in a ball at the foot of her bed each night. She is there right on Faith's heels as she comes home from school each day. Noel knows to whom she belongs and every person in our home can witness that knowledge any given day. We also have a dog, Gable. He is our rescue greyhound that we adopted almost two years ago from a local racetrack. Although he weighs four times her weight, and stands eye to eye with her, Hope has become his biggest fan. Lately, Hope has been feeling a little envious of the fact that Faith has a sense of ownership of a pet in our home that she does not have. Hope loves Gable, plays with Gable, loves to give Gable treats and hold his leash when we take him outside, but she never knew what it was to "own" Gable, to have the sense that he belongs to her. That is until the day that she asked me if he could be *her* dog. Of course, I thought it was only fair, since Faith had a cat, to let Hope have a sense of ownership of our dog. A whole new realm of experience has opened up to her as she now interacts with Gable as *her* dog. No more do I have to feed him; she is right there to supervise that he is getting enough food. No longer do I have to search all over the house for Gable's leash; Hope knows exactly where it is and is often using it to take him for walks through the house. Today I even caught her trying to brush his teeth with her own toothbrush!

Hope's awareness of her ownership of Gable has made a huge difference in not only her life, but in her confidence as well. Sometimes we don't realize just what it is to take *ownership* of something until we have experienced it for ourselves.

Today we will spend some time with David as we witness the day that perhaps inspired his words in Psalm 23:5(b), "You anoint my head with oil; my cup overflows."

Please join me in 1 Samuel 16:1-13. After reading the verses, answer the questions below.

> In verse 1, whom does God say He has provided a king for?

> Where did Samuel go (verse 4)?

I love how perfect God's plans are. Long before any man knew of Christ's coming, God knew and made sure that David was living there at just the right time that he was to be anointed king of Israel. God was foreshadowing the coming of a greater king, the King of kings who would one day come to be born in Bethlehem, the house of God.

> Who did Samuel think was surely the "one" God has chosen (verse 6)?

What does God say about how He chooses who will become king (verse 7)?

According to verses 10-12, which son had God chosen to be His king?

This is significant because the youngest son was often seen as the least in the eyes of Israelite families. Tending sheep was the least respected job of the Israelite home. For God to choose "the least" shows so much about who and how He choose those who will come to serve in leadership for Him.

Does this characteristic of God surprise you in any way? If so, how?

To anoint David as king, Samuel would have opened a horn full of very special and expensive oil and then poured the whole horn over the head of David. There would be a fragrance in this oil that was specifically mixed for this anointing. Anointing was symbolic of the qualifications divinely imparted in the consecration of the persons (Vines, p. 18). The perfect fulfillment of this is displayed in verse 13.

What does it say in that verse "rushed upon David from that day forward?"

Does this passage of Scripture say anything about David's change in circumstances after this anointing took place?

We know that David's circumstances did not change after this anointing took place. He went back out into the fields and tended his sheep, perhaps maybe even things became worse for David as his envious brothers took out their frustrations of not being chosen on David. I can imagine him being teased more with comments such as, "David, how does it feel to be king of sheep?" or, "David, here is more work for you to do, we've got to prepare you for the day you will rule us all." I can imagine that there were many times out in the fields when David questioned his own destiny. Perhaps, at those moments, God would send a gentle breeze past the fields where David stood that would cause the remnant of the anointing oil's fragrance to come to life again and remind David that he was set apart for God. It is said that of all our senses, our sense of smell is the most powerful at associating us with past memories. I find it precious that God left David with a reminder of His grace for him through his sense of smell. Long after rains had washed away the oil from David's hair, perhaps some part of his clothing would still carry the scent that reminded David that he was more than what his circumstances might deem him at the moment. He belonged to God.

> Is there anything that you have that reminds you that you belong to God? Perhaps it is a tangible object or just a precious memory of a past experience. Please share it with us below.

There is another example in Scripture of an anointing that took place. Please meet me in John 12:1-8. After reading this account, please answer the questions below.

> When did this anointing take place?

> Who was it that "anointed" Jesus?

> What does verse 3 say about what happened in the room as this anointing took place? What special act of humility did Mary do for Jesus?

What does Jesus say about what Mary had done?

Does what Christ says about Mary's actions clue you in to what Mary understood about the sacrifice that Christ was going to make?

If we were to read this account in the book of Mark 14:3-9, we would see that Mary "broke the flask and poured it over his head," (v. 3). Six days before Jesus was to "break" His own body open for us and pour His life out over our heads, Mary performed this amazing act of servanthood and gratitude for our Savior. The flask was broken, with no way to save any of her greatest treasure for herself for later use in her life when she might need the security that this ointment represented to her. When she broke the flask, Christ saw more than what anyone else could see. He saw this women who was willing to pour all of her hope, all of her security, all of her "self" out for Him. Six days before He would reciprocate her generous act, by faith, she displayed exactly what it is that Christ seeks from each of us. I find it interesting that this act happened on the sixth day before His sacrifice. In the Bible, the number six represents man. It is almost as if her act is laying a drawbridge down by which Christ will allow us all to walk across from man and death to Himself and life. I love that she not only pours the oil out on His head, but then, as the oil drips to his feet, she begins to wash His feet with her hair. This was an amazing act of humility, yet if we look closely, we can see so much more. In the Bible, a woman's hair represents her glory (1 Cor.11:14-15). As she washed the feet of Christ, the very feet that were about to be pierced for her transgressions, she laid any and all of her glory down at His feet. As the oil dripping from His feet soaked in to her hair, there was an acknowledgment and exchange that took place between her heart and Christ's that only the two of them understood. In essence she was saying, "Jesus, I give you all my glory. I see You; I acknowledge You as my Glory. You as my worth, and from now on, Your fragrance will be mine and I will share You with the world. I would rather spend all my life washing your feet than seeking after my own glory. I see You, Jesus, and I know Your worth."

What kind of response, if any, does this picture illicit in you? Please share below.

There is another aspect of this exchange that is a foreshadow of what was about to take place.

Let's discover this amazing aspect of this exchange together. Please turn your Bibles to Genesis 3:14-15. After reading, make note of any comparisons you can draw from this judgment on the serpent and the act that Mary performed on Jesus six days before His sacrifice.

In the beginning of the curse, God pronounced that there would be enmity between the woman and the serpent. That her offspring shall bruise his head, and that he (the serpent) would bruise his heel. As Mary bent down to wash the feet of Christ with her hair, perhaps, without even knowing it, she was fulfilling the reversal of this very judgment on all mankind. The very feet that would soon wear our curse would also crush, once and for all, the head of the enemy. Six days after this amazing interaction transpired, Mary could still smell the fragrance that lingered on her head, unaware that the very feet that also shared her fragrance were crushing the head of the enemy that had us all bound. Perhaps Christ thought of this, too, as He endured the beatings and experienced the full rejection of the sheep whom He loved and came to save. Perhaps each time He became weak in His flesh, God would, by grace, send a breeze to blow the fragrance of Mary's sacrifice into the nostrils of our Lamb to help Him remember and endure.

Just as the oil flowed, allowing David to experience what it was to *belong* to God, so Mary's anointing was an amazing display that she had chosen to *belong* to Christ, and amazingly, He chose to *belong* to her, and to each of us who is willing to allow Him to anoint us through the blood of His sacrifice. For each of us who belong to Him, there was a moment in heaven when Jesus came to you, looked up at the Father with a smile and said, "Rise, anoint her, for this is the one." (Based on 1 Samuel 16:12(b)).

Let's close in a prayer thanking our Shepherd for choosing us, and receiving once again the anointing of His amazing love. Good job, girls!

Week 4

The Valley of The Shadow of Death

Fill in the blanks below with the words according to the lesson valley, sacrifice,
truth, Present, transferring, others, weight, living, manage, perfected

Romans 12:1-2, "*I appeal to you therefore, brothers, by the mercies of God, to present your bodies as a living sacrifice, holy and acceptable to God, which is your spiritual worship. Do not be conformed to this world, but be transformed by the renewal of your mind, that by testing you may discern what is the will of God, what is good and acceptable and perfect.*"

_____ your body as a _____ _____.

Faith = Taking the _____ off of you and _____ it on to GOD.

We will never know the truth of _____, only the _____ of the shadow of it.

We cannot _____ sin, we must crucify it.

The valley is where we find _____ Christ sends for us to identify with and minister to.

We are _____ through suffering, just as Jesus was.

Notes_____
_____
_____
_____
_____
_____
_____
_____
_____

Day 1

Surely Goodness And Mercy Shall Follow Me

DAILY GRAIN	Please begin by prayerfully receiving God's Word to you through these Scriptures: *"Surely goodness and mercy shall follow me ..." Psalm 23:6(a)* *"You hem me in, behind and before, and lay your hand upon me" Psalm 139:5*

I had to admit, this was fun! It was our first time out on *our* boat: a "hurricane boat" that my husband had bought for steal after Hurricane Ike hit our area and damaged many homes and boats (among other things). It was not until now, a year and half later, that the boat repairs had been made and we were ready to hit the water. As the boat sailed across the water, I began to think back with regret over all the times I nagged my husband about how much time he was spending outside working on the boat. He had bought it so our family could have something fun to do that spanned all of the age gaps in our children and that involved being outside. We are not wealthy family, so had we not been able to purchase our "Hurricane Ike fixer-upper," we might never have been able to afford to experience something like this as a family. As we whizzed by the million dollar homes and the other expensive boats out on the lake with all of their bells and whistles, I felt like I was a new member of some club where I did not really fit in. However, as we sped faster and faster out on the open water and the homes and other boats drifted into the distance, I began to see fish jumping out of the blue and green abyss, pelicans swooping down to catch mouthfuls of water, and the seagulls dip and dive towards each other in playful wonder. I realized then that this boat ride was more than a chance encounter with those who have more money and more toys than we do; it was a chance for God to show me a whole new chapter of His creation up close. My heart bubbled over with gratitude as the tears of joy mixed with the droplets of water that were streaming across my face. I could almost hear God saying, "Don't you just love it? I made this day just for you and your family to enjoy!" His goodness was all around me, impossible to miss. My shepherd had led me in to a broad place and I was having such a blast!

> Have you ever had a day or moment like this, one that you knew that God had almost wrapped up as a gift just for you? Please share about it below.

It was an amazing day, however, like everything here in Earth, it was not perfect. The heat was as is normal in Texas summers: unbearable. As the boat sped up, I was grateful for the sudden gush of wind and little droplets of water that would breeze past me, allowing some reprieve from the sun's scorching rays. However, it was not long before my escape from the dangerous heat was replaced by a new danger: the danger of one of my girls falling overboard as the now speeding boat bounced and rocked along the ever-changing current. My heart nearly skipped a beat as I noticed from the back of the boat where I was perched, Hope's (my four year old) feet move from the ice chest where she had them propped up. She and Faith, our eight year old, where sitting together on a bench just in front of where my husband stood steering the boat. From my seat, I could only see their feet and the very top of their hair as it bounced in the wind just above my husband's wind visor. My heart nearly leapt out of my chest as I saw her peer around where my husband stood with his back towards me. If she tried to walk back towards me, she could have easily been knocked overboard by the boat's continuous bouncing on the waves. As I saw that, I'm-coming-and-no-one-can-stop-me look in her eyes, I screamed for my husband to slow down just in time for her to make a dash for my now open arms. As I swooped her up and wrapped my arms around her tight, I could feel her melt into me and realized that she must have been afraid up in the front of the boat, so exposed and vulnerable with no one big to hold onto if she was rocked or bounced off of her bench. Like a 3-D movie screen, the image of today's Scripture began to come close enough for me to touch. "Surely goodness and mercy shall follow me …" Psalm 23:6(a). I could see how God's goodness allowed me to come onto the boat, to experience something new that He has not shown me before, yet His mercy is here too. It is His mercy that knows exactly what our boundaries are, how much we can stand in these new places that He leads us to. Just as my daughter, Hope, needed to be held onto tight through this experience in order for me to protect her from the possible dangers that she could unknowingly bring upon herself through her thoughtless actions, so I too need God to "hold me tight" through some of the experiences that He walks me through in life. Only He knows my true limitations, and in His *mercy*, He inflicts boundaries on me sometimes that I may not like or understand. He knows how much freedom it will take before I get myself bounced overboard as I experience the rocking waves that always tend to find us through this journey through life. He is good enough to want us to know what it is to experience the amazing aspects of life that are found only in Him, yet merciful enough to know just what we can take and how to instill boundaries in our lives to keep us from causing our own destruction. "Surely goodness and mercy shall follow you …" (Psalm 23:6 (a), personalization mine), when you follow the Shepherd, goodness and mercy can't help but follow you.

Let's get to our main text for today where we will look more closely in to this aspect of our good Shepherd.

Please meet me in John 10:1-18. After reading, please answer the questions below.

According to verses 1-2, how is the Shepherd known?

In Christ's day, shepherds often kept their sheep together at night in a fenced enclosure that had only one entrance. There would be a shepherd that would act as the watchman at night and he would lay his body across the entrance and would only let the shepherds of those sheep into the fold. Sometimes, thieves or predators would try and break through the fence to steal or kill the sheep inside.

According to verses 3-5, how does Christ lead his sheep out?

Have you ever experienced Christ, "leading you out?" If so, what was that experience like? If not, what do you feel might be prohibiting you?

In verse 9, Christ describes 3 actions that happen to us when we are led by Him. What are they? Do you have any life experiences that relate to Christ's words?

Verse 10 is one of the most famous verses in the New Testament. Please make these words personal by adding your name in the blanks below.

"The thief comes only to steal and kill and destroy _____. *But I came that* _____ *may have life and have it abundantly. John 10:10*

> In verses 11-15, Jesus is describing the difference between the "Good Shepherd" and a "hired hand." What does He say the differences are?

> Have you ever experienced a "hired hand fleeing" when the wolves have come to "snatch you?" If so, share about that experience below.

I know that I have experienced those whom I have trusted to keep me safe, fleeing from me when trouble has come. I am ashamed to admit it, but I have also been like one of the hired hands that have fled when trouble has come. Sometimes it is hard to know how to respond when people we know and care about are hurting. Some of our natural instincts involve just avoiding them in hopes that we don't have to experience the awkwardness of not having an answer for what they are going through. One of the true marks of Christian maturity is when we can't stay away when those around us are hurting. We will begin to stop trying to find the right answer and instead will allow Christ to make us the right answer. After a while of being shepherded by Him, we can't help but learn to behave like Him.

> What about you, have you ever been like one of the "hired hands" that flees from those around you when the wolf has come?

> In verse 16, how many flocks and how many shepherds are there?

When we were out on the boat, Christ showed me another aspect of His "goodness and mercy." After a while of being out on the water, my husband asked Joshua, our fifteen year old, if he would like to help him with the boat. Josh was able to not only help in steering the boat when we came in to dock, but also helped in securing the boat to the dock and even loading the boat back on the trailer (which was pretty exciting). I could see how Josh's demeanor changed as he went from being just a passenger on the boat to being one of its captains. In the same way, once our Shepherd has grown us in to a place of maturity in Himself, He not only lets us experience the loving care that He offers us as our Shepherd, but He lets us join Him in doing what He does: shepherding others. We who are sheep get to also be shepherds! How cool is that? In this way, just as John 10:16 says, we are able to be, "one flock, with one shepherd." Sheep must learn to believe and trust that their shepherd has good things in store for them and that, in his mercy, he is looking out for their own protection. As this trust in their shepherd builds and increases, so they are able to take their eyes off of their own "grass-eating agenda" and onto their shepherd. They know that, if he is moving them, it is for their own best interests. As they watch him, they are able to know when it is time to move on and when it is time to lie down and rest. They know that he will feed them if grass is sparse so they do not worry when the fields look dry. Slowly but surely, these sheep become "one" with their shepherd. They learn him, and they can tell by his voice what his intentions are and they respond. As their focus is trained upward on their shepherd, their vision for their lives is expanded outward. Their mouths no longer lead their hearts, for they have learned that their hearts are safest with their shepherd. Once we are at this place with our Shepherd, He is able to entrust us with His greatest treasure, His sheep. In Matthew 20:26-28, Christ says, "Whoever would be great among you must be your servant, and whoever would be first among you must be your slave, even as the Son of Man came not to be served but to serve and to give his life as a ransom for many." We are never more "one" with our Shepherd than when we are at His side, serving and shepherding His sheep. One flock, one Shepherd, one church. I can see it now, just as Psalm 139:5 says, "You hem me in, behind and before, and lay your hand upon me." Jesus picks us up in His mercy and trains us to follow Him to the "good pastures" here in Earth, the places where we are most nourished in His truth. As He entrusts us with this journey, He leans over us and leads to the good places with one hand, while in His mercy, placing the other hand behind us for protection. His body is our covering, and as we follow Him, we literally leave a trail of His goodness and mercy behind for the whole world to see.

Please close in a prayer today thanking Him for His goodness and mercy towards you.

Sheep's Blood Still the Answer

I find it both beautiful and awesome how literal God's Word proves to be. As I studied sheep, I was shocked to find that there are sheep being raised today for the sole purpose of using their blood for biomedical reasons. The medical community has discovered that sheep's blood is the best form of culture media to use in isolating microorganisms as well as in helping to diagnose infections. It is even used to help produce antibodies against snake venom.

There are two scriptures that sprang to mind as I ran across this information;

> *Genesis 3:15, "I will put enmity between you and the woman, and between your offspring and her offspring; he shall bruise your head, and you shall bruise his heel."*

> *Exodus 12:13, "The blood shall be a sign for you, on the houses where you are. And when I see the blood, I will pass over you, and no plague will befall you to destroy you, when I strike the land of Egypt."*

It will bless you if you go back and read the passages surrounding these scriptures, and if you do, you will discover there are some common themes.

The one we will discuss today is the theme of separation.

SEPARATION...POWERFUL WORD! What immediate memories, words, or experiences come to mind as you think upon that word.

If you are like me, this word goes back a long way and is associated with many painful memories. You may be wondering at this point, "What does separation, sheep's blood, and sickness have to do with anything?"

It all comes together in John 10, let's read the whole chapter together and see if we can figure it out.

> *John 10:9-10, "I am the door. If anyone enters by me, he will be saved and will go in and out and find pasture. The thief comes only to steal and kill and destroy. I came that they may have life and have it abundantly,"*

For each of us, there are moments, sometimes they come many times throughout each day. Moments when we have our heels bruised by sin in this world, and moments when we are plagued by our own sins or the sins of others. We feel alone, separate from God and one another. We want to hide in these moments. But, there remains a blood-stained door that we can walk through, *"when I see the BLOOD, I will pass over you, and no plague will befall you or destroy you." (Exodus 12:13), "I came that they may have life and have it abundantly."*

Just as the lamb's blood is used today to isolate and diagnose where infections are hiding, so Christ's blood is able to isolate that which isolates us from Him and one another. His blood never fails to bring His sheep back home, and to heal what the enemy's venom has poisoned in our lives and families.

Day 2

Surely Goodness And Mercy Shall Follow Me

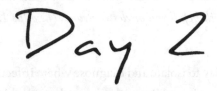

DAILY GRAIN	Please begin by prayerfully receiving God's Word to you through these Scriptures: *"Surely goodness and mercy shall follow me ..." Psalm 23:6(a)* *"He will again have compassion on us; he will tread our iniquities underfoot. You will cast our sins into the depths of the sea." Micah 7:19*

There is still a grayish, purple stain there as a reminder. I love blackberry cobbler; it is one of my favorite desserts in the world. Less than a month after we had new carpet installed in our children's rooms, I happened to be enjoying a bowl of this heaven-sent sweetness when I noticed that it was time to get my girls in bed. Afraid that my husband might mistake my temporary absence from my bowl as an indication that I was done eating it, I decided to take it with me into my girls' bedroom as I put them to bed. After sitting it on the side of their toy chest, I began reading the girls their bed-time stories, unaware that our cat had entered the room and was finding the smell of my heavenly dessert to be as irresistible as it truly was. My girls suddenly gasp as they saw the bowl topple over and slam the dark purple and red filling all over the new carpet. I almost had to laugh at myself for my own misplaced anger over the loss of my dessert over the now huge stain setting in to our brand new carpet. After rubbing and scrubbing so much that my skin became raw, I realized that I was never going to get that stain fully out. The blackberries had made their mark on our carpet, and that mark would be there until we moved or replaced the carpet.

Just as those blackberries left a permanent stain on my carpet, so our Shepherd leaves a permanent stain on our hearts, and if we let Him, that stain can extend to those who will follow in our footsteps. Just as a tar truck leaves the smoothed out, black trail of newly paved roads, so the stain of Christ's goodness and mercy will literally follow us all the days of our lives.

So, how does this happen? How do we allow our Shepherd to "stain" our lives in such a way that we leave a legacy for those who will follow us?

Let's look at Micah 7:1-8 and see if we can gain some insight into this.

After reading Micah 7:1-8, please answer the following questions below.

In verse 1, what is Micah comparing himself to?

Do you ever feel lonely in your search for the righteous, the "summer fruit?" If so, how do you deal with your loneliness in seeking Christ in such a dry land?

Verses 2-6 describe with vivid accuracy so much of what is happening in our world today. It amazes me how timeless God's Word is. Since the Fall, men have been sinners; therefore, the outward actions of men have not changed so much that we cannot relate today in our current society.

In verses 2-6, which stand out to you the most as being one that directly affects your life?

There are a few that stand out to me as struggles that I deal with. "Each hunts the other with a net." So often we perceive that others are trying to "catch us" in our words and actions. Especially when we are Christians, there seems to be a "net" that is always out to catch us in our imperfections so that we can be portrayed as hypocrites. The enemy will often use this too, as we move from abiding in Christ, who is our perfection, to trying to avoid a list of mistakes. This then becomes the net we will always fall into. The moment our walk with Christ becomes about something measurable, we have moved out of the abundance of His Presence and do not stand a chance. I think that Oswald Chambers described this best when he said, "If we have a purpose of our own, it destroys the simplicity and leisureliness which ought to characterize the children of God" (My Utmost for His Highest, Aug.5th).

The other one that stood out to me was the word "confusion." This word describes how I often feel as I seek to follow my Shepherd through this world. The day my confusion is surely at hand is when I allow the currents of this world to skew my vision of simply walking with my Shepherd. One sign that I need to be reoriented in Him is when I begin to experience confusion. He is always showing us the way, so we can always trust Him to guide us back when the path of righteousness begins to become fuzzy due to the constant bombardment of the world on our senses.

Verses 7 and 8 speak of this. What does verse 8 say that he (Micah) will do?

What does it say God will do?

Verse 8 follows this with one of my favorite verses: "Rejoice not over me. O my enemy; when I fall. I shall rise; when I sit in darkness, the LORD will be a light to me." This verse presents us with the picture of perseverance that is ours in Christ. We will fall, but in Him, we will never stay down. God is always shining His light onto the next place, the next part of the Promised Land He is calling us to conquer, and He, Himself, ensures that we will rise each time. If we skip down to Micah 7:18-19, we can see exactly how our Shepherd is able to deliver us.

Let's read Micah 7:18-19 together and then answer the questions below.

What does verse 18 say that God delights in?

What does verse 19 say He will do with our sins?

"He will again have compassion on us, He will tread our iniquities under foot …" (Micah 7:19). We have looked at the topic of feet before in our study, and today we will consider them again as we seek to gain true awareness of what it takes to leave a stain of goodness and mercy behind us.

Head to the following verses and record below what each says about our iniquities, walking, or feet.

Isaiah 53:4-5

Genesis 3:15

Matthew 27:31

Long ago, our Shepherd decided to wear our stain of sin on Himself. Just as blackberries must be crushed to allow the juice to come out, and the heat to allow the cohesion to take place that make blackberries into blackberry cobbler, so Christ underwent the heat of Hell's flames, and the crushing of His body so that He might be able to leave the stain of His blood on each of our lives. It is the stain of His blood that allows us to leave behind a stain on the lives of others. Just as the cobbler left a stain that could not be removed on my carpet, so we as Christians leave the stain of Christ on the lives of all of those in our realm of influence as we truly walk in obedience to Him. We don't have to do anything but allow Him to make us someone He can serve to the whole world, a heavenly dessert whose aroma draws all men to want to taste and see. In order for Christ to pour Himself into us, He must make room in our hearts by crushing the self out of us. Just as a winepress squeezes grapes to produce wine, and just as a farmer must till up the hard soil on top to reach the fertile soil underneath when planting his harvest, so Christ takes those very same nail-pierced feet that tread over the head of the enemy, and walks around in our hearts, crushing all that keeps us from being able to fully trust Him. As He treads over all of the hardened places in our hearts, He pours Himself in until we are overflowing, leaving a trail of His goodness and mercy on this world and in the hearts of others.

> In what ways do you sense that Christ is "treading over" your heart right now, or tilling up some "hardened soil?"

Let Him, Sweet One, let Him squeeze you out, cook you up, and serve you to this world as you become more and more His. In closing, I am going to share a poem that I wrote during my own season of being "tread over." I hope you enjoy it. After reading, please close in a prayer of gratitude for all of the stains that He allows us to leave on the hearts of others.

The Joy of Being Caught

"He who is bowed down shall speedily be released …" Isaiah 51:14

"And I have put My words in your mouth and covered you in the shadow of My Hand, establishing the heavens and laying the foundations of the earth and saying to Zion, "You are My people" ' Isaiah 51:16

Come tread the carnal places Lord
Etched upon my soul
Turn the tables over my King
Fill in every hole

Come tear down all the walls I've built
Leave no stone unturned
Till up all the fallow ground
Till Your Truth is all I yearn

Then plunge Your Holy hands in me
Till every piece is torn apart
And all that there is left of me
Is the fertile soil of a new heart

Then tread over me once more My King
Crush me under Holy feet
Till all that there ever was of me
Is Holy obsolete

Then come plant Your garden here
In what is left of me
That precious fruit may nourish souls
And change eternity

And if a weed called "self" should sneak
Into this garden You adore
Till up the fallow ground again
Tread over me once more

Crush me under Holy feet
Till there's no more me
Or until my feet tread Holy soil
For all eternity

Day 3

Surely Goodness And Mercy Shall Follow Me

DAILY GRAIN	Please begin by prayerfully receiving God's Word to you through these Scriptures: *"…shall follow me all the days of my life, and I shall dwell in the house of the LORD …" Psalm 23:6(b)* *"The Spirit gives life; the flesh counts for nothing. The words I have spoken to you are spirit and life. Yet there are some of you who do not believe." John 6:63-64NIV*

My girls were just in time-out for fighting (again). It seems to always go the same way. Faith resists going until I give her an ultimatum and Hope cries and cries, as if it is the end of the world to have to stop what she is doing for a few minutes to consider her behavior. When the time is up and I do my best impression of the Super Nanny in reminding them of the reasons they were in time out, encourage them to make better choices next time, and then let them know that their time is up and they are free. Hope always comes out and gives me a hug and tells me that she loves me, while Faith hides her face and defiantly stays in the same place. I remind her that I love her, and that she is free to go as she grunts and slumps even lower into her time-out chair. She chooses to stay in place, to restrict herself in an effort to get at me. She does not realize that she is the only one who is losing out through her choice of not entering back in to the freedom she has been given. So often, we are the ones choosing to dwell in "time-out" and don't even realize it.

There are so many definitions for the word "dwell" in the Bible that it would take me this whole lesson to expand on them all. For today, we will hone in on the definition that fits in our text for today. It is found in John 6:56 where Jesus says, "Whoever eats my flesh and drinks my blood remains in me, and I in them." The word "remains" in Greek is MENO, and it means to abide, to remain, to dwell. Back in Week 3, we looked into a story about Elijah as he was on the Mountain of God after he had been running from Jezebel who was seeking to kill him. On the mountain, God asked him the question, "what are you doing here?"(1 Kings 19:13). We see God asking a similar question in Genesis 3:9 right after Adam and Eve ate the apple that sealed the fate for all of us. After hiding in the trees from God, He calls out to them, "where are you?" Today we will look in to a hard teaching of Christ that will demand us to ask ourselves the same question, "Where are you? Where are you dwelling?"

There are times that walking with Jesus will require us to examine our hearts in ways that might be challenging for us. Just as the teaching we will look into today does, there are times when Christ cuts to the chase of what our intentions are. Let's meet Him and His disciples in John 6:27-70. This account that we are looking into happened right after Jesus fed the 5,000. There were many people who followed Him after witnessing this miracle and these make up the audience for which He is speaking to in the following verses.

After reading John 6:27-70, please answer the following questions.

In verses 27-29, Christ is pointing the people towards what? What does Jesus say that the "work of God is?"

In verses 30-34, what are the people seeking from Christ and how does He respond?

In verses 35-40, who does Jesus say He is and for what purpose does He say He came?

Based the people's response in verses 41-42, did the people reject or receive Christ's words?

What part of what Christ said did they reject?

In verses 43-47, Christ is talking about who has eternal life and how they get it. How do we come to eternal life based on Christ's words here?

In 48-51, what is Christ calling Himself?

How do you respond to Christ's claim that He is the "bread of life?" What do you believe He means by this?

In verses 52-59, Jesus proclaims some of the most controversial statements in His ministry up until that point. As I tried to imagine what it must have been like for those people to hear those statements come from a man who they did not know how to perceive, I can only imagine that my response might not have been that different from theirs. I cannot imagine how some mere man could ask me to "feed on His flesh, and to drink His blood," to experience eternal life. Maybe today, in light of our society's recent vampire obsession, it may go over a little bit better than it did back then. We must remember that Christ was speaking to Israelites who were taught the law from their earliest years, which specifically forbade them from eating any animal that was unclean and considered anyone who touched a bodily fluid (including blood) unclean.

Try to imagine that you were part of Christ's audience on that day. From their side of the cross, what do you think might have been your response to Christ's words?

There are some very telling questions that are asked in verses 60-70. In the space below, record each question that is asked whether it is a direct question or implied, making note of who is asking it.

Now, go back to each of the questions above, and after praying, answer them according to what Christ is laying on your heart right now.

My heart beats faster as I picture the encounter between Christ and His disciples that takes place in verses 67-68. Most of Christ's disciples left right there in that moment. They were people who had watched Christ perform amazing miracles, listened to John's proclamation that He is "The Christ," and left everything to follow Him. These people left everything because they truly believed that He was their Savior, the Messiah, the Christ, the Promised One. For them to walk away was no easy feat. Like a sifter coming down from Heaven, Christ words cut right to their hearts, revealing the truth of their own belief in this man they had left everything to follow. As they walked away, the twelve stayed, maybe they did not even understand why their feet stayed planted right there next to Christ. Then Christ's words cut through the intensity like a knife, "You do not want to leave too, do you?," and then Peter speaks up, despite himself and says, "LORD, to whom shall we go? You have the words of eternal life. We have come to **believe** and to **know** that You are the Holy One of God." (John 6:68. Emphasis mine).

Have Christ's words ever become "a hard teaching" for you to hear? If so, what has become hard for you to hear and how are you responding to His truth?

At some point, we are all going to come to that place where God asks us, "where are you?" Just as the knife of Christ's words pierced through the hearts of these disciples, it pierces through our hearts as we come to see the line in the sand that He is asking us to walk across. To go forward with Him might mean that we must walk away from the life that we wanted to claim here on Earth. To walk forward could mean that we are walking with a Christ, a Messiah, who looks much different from the idealistic version of the god we had envisioned Him to be. At some point, like Elijah, God asks us the hard question: "what are you doing here?" And we know that our answer to this question will determine our entire destiny. Where are we? Are we going to live in the world, or are we going to live in Christ?

As we close today, let's have a real conversation with God as we allow Him to show us the truth about where our hearts are dwelling.

> Write your name next to the Scripture question below and then pray for God to show you the truth about the answer. Write your response below.

"What are you doing here_____?" (based on 1 Kings 19:13).

Jesus says, "The Spirit gives life; the flesh counts for nothing. The words I have spoken to you-they are full of the Spirit and life" (John 6:63). Each time we stop dwelling in Christ, we are giving ourselves a "time-out" from Life. Don't lose out on life, Sweet One, by wasting it sitting in "time-out." He has come to give you life! So dwell in it!

WEEK 5 BECOMING EWE

Day 4

Surely Goodness And Mercy Shall Follow Me

<table>
<tr>
<td>DAILY GRAIN </td>
<td>Please begin by prayerfully receiving God's Word to you through these Scriptures:

"...shall follow me all the days of my life, and I shall dwell in the house of the Lord forever." Psalm 23:6(b)

"And when he had spent everything, a severe famine arose in that country, and he began to be in need." Luke 15:14</td>
</tr>
</table>

There are a few times in our walk with Christ when He allows us to see tangible ways in which He has changed our hearts spiritually. So often we take all that He has done in our lives, hearts, and circumstances for granted because, like sheep, we are focused on what is right in front of us and we seldom see the larger picture of all He is doing inside of us. We want to *see* so badly that we forget that He must often move many mountains inside of us and others before evidence becomes visible on the outside. However, there are times when those mountains He is moving are so big that our hearts rejoice in wonder when we get to experience the weightlessness of their disappearance.

The time I have spent with the homeless has represented a huge mountain that Christ has moved in my heart. There was a time when I was terrified of interacting with someone who was homeless. It wasn't so much that I was terrified of them, but it was more that I was afraid of what they represented to me. I am a caregiver and love to help others as much as I can; however, the needs of so many of the homeless are so great that they overwhelm me with reminders of my own inability to truly help. Like neon signs blinking in the dark of night, their presence has always taunted me with questions about my own belief in Christ and in myself. I saw each time I was confronted with a homeless person as a confrontation with Christ Himself, as if He were saying, "Do you truly love Me, Rhonda?" Like a pop-quiz on loving that I was seldom prepared to take, I began to avoid them in hopes that I could avoid the truth about myself. In reality, they represented a part of my life that I was not ready to deal with yet. The part of me that believes that my own wit, resources, and courage are what have allowed me to not be *like* them. The part of me that believes that I am better than them, that they are weaker than me, and because of that, they deserve the circumstances that they are in. The part of me that much resembles the big brother in the parable that we will spend our last two days together looking at, the parable of the prodigal son.

Please turn with me to Luke 14:1-6, 14:25, 15:1-2 and 15:11-16. After reading these verses, please answer the questions below.

> Who was Christ telling these parables to? What do you think the atmosphere
> was like as He was telling them (verses 14:1-6, 14:25, 15:1-2)?

To the Pharisees, the Sabbath was a day of "what not to do." It represented the day of the week that was hardest to keep, and also the one day where you could easily "bust" someone for breaking the "law" that God had set in place. What God had given them as a gift of rest, they had perverted in to a legalistic way of setting themselves apart from the rest of mankind. Notice how, in verse 14:1, they were "watching [Christ] carefully." They were not watching because they believed He was God and wanted to learn from Him, they were watching for a way to "bust" Him. Like four-year-old tattle tales, they wanted to get Him in trouble because, like all of us sheep so often do, they would rather take down the truth than admit that they were wrong and needed to change.

I love how verse 15:1 says that, "the tax collectors and sinners were all drawing near to hear him." While Christ was getting sneers and rolled eyes from one half of the audience, the other half was finding something that they never thought was available to them through the words of this mystery man: hope, hope that maybe God loved them too.

> Based on verse 15:12, what do you feel was the younger son's attitude towards
> his father?

Based on verses 12-13, how did the father respond to his younger son's request?

For the father to give this son his share of the estate was no easy feat. This usually did not happen until the father was near death when he would give his blessing to his sons as he passed on his inheritance to them. For the son to ask for his share meant that he was not interested in the blessing or in sticking around to take care of the estate. The father withheld his right to maintain his authority over the estate so that he could grant his son the freedom to choose what he wanted to do with all that his father had provided for him. How often we overlook all the ways our Father and Shepherd has proved His love for us through offering us the freedom in which to choose what we will do with all that He has given us. Will we "squander it on reckless living," or will we honor Him through seeking His blessing and desires for our lives?

> Verses 14-16 depict a scene that hits home for me in so many ways. What kind of animal was the younger son sent to feed?

In Leviticus 11:7, God gives specific instructions to the Israelites to stay away from pigs. He calls them unclean and instructs them not to eat them or touch their carcasses. For this Jewish man to have taken this job shows his utter desperation and destitution. He is now in the presence of what he has been taught all of his life to be "unclean." So often, we as Christians find ourselves in the same condition.

> When was the last time you can recall being the midst of what you knew in your heart to be "unclean?"

It doesn't take long for me to find myself in the "pig-pens" of this world. Each day ushers in new challenges for me to stay out of the pig-pens. One of the most difficult challenges that I am currently facing deals with my own propensity to experience bitterness over anything I perceive encroaches upon my thoughts of how I believe things should go. In my perfect world, everyone is nice to one another, everyone gets along, people are always offering to help me with all of the chores that I must do each day, people are always noticing all that I do for them and thanking me constantly, my husband always dotes on me as he offers to take the kids so that I can have a day of rest, and no one is ever late or in a bad mood. Wow, it really ticks me off when people mess up my "perfect world." I am trying to learn to be more like Christ in my ability to exit Rhonda and just enter into Christ's ability to love people right where they are at, right in the midst of all the ways they are encroaching on my perfect world. I am really trying to lay down my expectations of everyone else at the foot of the cross and to hang up my desire for a "perfect world," in exchange for a desire to be more like my perfect Savior.

We end with verse 16, where our prodigal is, "longing to be fed with the pods that the pigs ate, but no one gave him anything." I find it almost funny how we so often see God's unwillingness to feed us while we are in our pig-pens as a lack of mercy on His part. From His perspective, He must see any type of sustenance we receive there as being something that will only prolong our stay in a place where He is separated from us and unable to love us and lead us towards true life and love. It is what we so often see as His lack of mercy that is actually His greatest mercy towards us. Each hunger pang we experience in our pig-pens presents a new opportunity for us to find our way home in to His arms.

> Right now, what are the pig-pens that you often find yourself in? What is keeping you from being nourished in Your Father's arms?

In 1 Corinthians 15:50, Paul says, "I declare to you, brothers and sisters, that flesh and blood cannot inherit the kingdom of God, not does the perishable inherit the imperishable." Each time we allow God to move us out of a pig-pen that we have found ourselves in, He is moving us out of what is perishable into what is imperishable. He is preparing us for our home in Heaven, where we will dwell in His house forever. Just as Christ has caused me to confront my beliefs about the homeless that had kept me from seeing the truth that I was in a "pig pen" that I was not ready to get out of, so He will show you the truth about your own pig-pens that are keeping you from going home with Him. In reality, we will never be "mud-free" until we find ourselves all the way home in God's kingdom, but we have a wonderful Savior and Shepherd who stays in the mud with us as long as it takes for us to realize that our real hunger is for Him.

Take some time closing in a prayer thanking Christ for His ability to Shepherd us, even in the pig-pens of life.

Day 5

Surely Goodness And Mercy Shall Follow Me

DAILY GRAIN	Please begin by prayerfully receiving God's Word to you through these Scriptures: *"…shall follow me all the days of my life, and I shall dwell in the house of the Lord forever" Psalm 23:6(b)* *"For this my son was dead, and is alive again; he was lost, and is found. And they began to celebrate." Luke 15:24*

It is raining really hard outside, and my own thoughts portray how much God has truly changed my heart. "Where are they? Are they under the bridge, safe from the rain? How I hope they were able to get their things to shelter before the rain started. I hope that this rain does not mean that the mosquitoes are going to begin swarming them again." A whole population of people who I refused to see before now riddle my mind and thoughts so often that I can't help but thank God for the gift that they are to me.

I will never forget the day when I first noticed that my heart had changed towards the homeless. I had been given a book for Christmas that I had heard many people talking about. I figured that it must be a good read, so I picked it up not realizing that in its pages laid a recipe that God had created to allow me to read my own heart. Through each chapter, I was able to see more and more how what I thought was a small speck of mud on myself was in reality a huge ocean that was separating me from fully experiencing the love and wonder of who God is. I began to realize that, like them, I am homeless. I wander through

RHONDA DE LA MORINIERE

this world in search for somewhere to belong, someone to acknowledge me and to be thankful that I was born, that I am here. Just as the homeless carry their earthly belongings with them everywhere they go in fear that someone will take them, so I carry what I perceive will make me seem valuable to the world around with me each day, afraid to lay it down, afraid that someone might remove it to reveal the true me hidden underneath. The truth that who they are is all they have, rings like a fire siren in my own soul. They live out literally the truth about us all: that once all our belongings and protections are stripped away, all we have is who we are. It is a terrifying thought if not for the knowledge that there is someone who makes who we are so much more than we often can see or imagine. Let's pick up in our parable we left off on yesterday to find out more about who this someone is.

Let's read through the rest of the parable in Luke 15:17-32. After you have finished, please answer the questions below.

> Verses 17-19 tender my heart as I imagine the veil being lifted from this poor son's eyes. Describe what is happening in this young man's awareness in these Scriptures. Is there a difference between the young man who left and the young man who wants to return now? What is it?

> What do the young man's reasons for returning appear to be? Are they emotional, spiritual, or circumstantial?

> What does verse 20 say about what the father was doing when the young boy returned?

> We can assume that the father had no idea when or even if his son would return, so what does his stance say about his heart towards his son?

In order for this father to "run towards him," he had to pull up the long robes he was wearing which was typical for men to wear at that time. This was not considered proper behavior for him. And then to "kiss and embrace" this son who was covered in pig slop — and who knows what else — would have rendered this father completely undignified.

> What does this father's behavior indicate about his reasons for his actions? Were they emotional, spiritual, or circumstantial?

> As we see the differences in the reasons for the actions between these two men, let's look at our own. When do we most often "return to our Father?" Are our reasons spiritual, emotional, or circumstantial?

It is humbling isn't it? I notice that, if I will truly listen to my Father and Shepherd, I can sense Him calling out to me in my heart and tugging at my emotions. However, more often than I would like to admit, I don't turn and make the long trek home until I am covered in the slop of this world and am seeking circumstantial change.

How safe and secure it makes my heart feel to know that, even when I am stubborn about coming home to Him, He is still ready to run and meet me as soon as I turn my heart homeward. The only time God is ever depicted as running in His Word is towards you and me.

> In verse 21, the son says his speech to his father. What does the son say about what he expects his relationship to be with his father at this point?

> And then in verses 22-24, what do the father's actions imply about his own expectations of what his relationship will now be with his son?

How often we do come back home, heads bowed, eyes to the floor, full of condemnation and shame, just hoping that maybe our Father will let us back in the door if we try really hard this time to not make another mistake. Or even more often, we come home, but feel as if we must enter a time of penance for our sins. We don't feel that we are worthy to be fully embraced and accepted by our Father again after all we have done. Yet, He never requires that from us. Romans 8:1 promises us that, "There is therefore now no condemnation for those who are in Christ Jesus." What an amazing Shepherd and Savior we have! The moment we turn, He slips His own robe over our shoulders, ready to cover up all of our mess from the world. He places His own ring on our finger, signifying His trust in us and His willingness to share His own glory and authority with us. He reaches down and places His own shoes on our feet, as He slips ours on His feet. He entrusts us with His ability to walk in the fullness of His promises, as He reminds us of His own willingness to have walked through every pig-pen we have ever been in, enabling us to walk in the victory that He has provided. Then He takes our arm and leads us back on the path towards life. We walk towards home with Him where, upon arrival, we will partake in the greatest homecoming party any of us have ever seen!

What does Revelation 19:6-9 reveal about the party we will attend one day when we get home?

Lastly, as we read verses 25-32, what do we discover about the older brother?

Does he express any excitement that his brother is alive and has come home?

What are your perceptions as to why the older brother is responding to the news of his younger brother's return?

Are there times when you struggle with being thankful for your brother's or sister's return home?

It is amazing how often we quantify whether or not someone is really ready to return home. We forget that we are the sheep, not the Shepherd. The moment we enter into judgment of others, we know we have left the pasture and are headed for a pig-pen.

Based on the verses you just read, does the brother ever enter into the celebration?

Why do you think that Christ leaves this piece of information out of His parable?

Now, going back to Luke 15:1-2, considering Christ's audience at the telling of this parable. Who are the "younger brothers" and who are the "older brothers?"

Looking at your own life, which brother are you?

Sister, who you are *is* all you have. What you do with who you are, in the end, is all that matters. Whether we choose to believe it or not, none of us is home yet. We are all homeless, on our way to a place that we have never seen with earthly eyes. However, as we allow Christ to continue His work in our hearts, allowing Him to shepherd our souls, we will catch glimpses of this home in our hearts. It may be in form of a passage of Scripture, a song with just the right words, the touch of a friend or loved one, or it may be in the eyes of a homeless man as you kneel down to place your hand on his knee and ask him how he has been. There are many places to go during our short time here on Earth. We sheep tend to stick close to whatever it is we are hungering for at any given moment of our lives. But, in the midst of our pastures, there stands a Shepherd who is willing to lead us out to new places, to places that will stretch us, challenge us, and teach us the truth about ourselves and our true purpose for being on Earth. His presence stands as a testament of His desire to give each of us, who are ready to admit our own homelessness, a home. Precious Lamb, may you be willing to allow these words to be your testimony: "Surely goodness and mercy shall follow me all the days of my life, and I shall dwell in the house of the Lord forever" Psalm 23:6.

Week 5

He Prepares a Table Before Me

Fill in the blanks below with the words according to the lesson path,
plans, tempt, holiness, sin, herd, staff, backward,

John 10:3, *"To him the gatekeeper opens. The sheep hear his voice, and he calls his own sheep by name and leads them out."*

Our hope is to identify with the One Who took_____ for us.

Christ has not given up on _____, so we can't either.

The enemy will often _____ us by giving us our own _____.

We must often go _____ in order to go forward.

Are you being deceived?

1. Want to blend in with _____ instead of snuggling up with the Shepherd.

2. Care more about individual _____ than God's purpose.

3. Follow a _____ instead of a Person (our Shepherd).

Notes_____
_____
_____

Stay in His Way

There is no easy way to finish a journey, not one that has been truly meaningful. How I pray that your ears perk ever more readily to the sound of your Shepherd's voice, that your eyes never cease to look for Him, even in life's seemingly most monotonous moments, and that your heart never fails to trust Him, even in life's most paralyzing moments. Our Shepherd never leaves our side.

There will be times when it becomes confusing to follow Him. Like sheep, our natural inclination will always be to watch the flock around us to follow. It is so easy to allow them to become our way instead of our Shepherd. If you take nothing else away from this study, please hear me on this. Never, ever forget to STAY IN HIS WAY. In John 14:6 Jesus says, "*I am the way, and the truth, and the life. No one comes to the Father except through me.*"

This whole world is so confused and confusing because it does not hear, nor understand what you and I now know, the Voice of the Shepherd. Even in the Church, there are those who take His grace for granted, and there are those who do not understand or accept His grace. We do them no favors by judging or condemning them. We can be miracles in their lives and show them Jesus as we simply STAY IN THE WAY (as JOHN 14:6 states), and pray for them according to God's word. As they see us walking in freedom, we shine His light to show them the Way to walk in it too.

That WAY is your home, Beloved, and one day, like Enoch (Genesis 5:24), you will lift up your eyes and realize that your precious sheep feet have walked right out of this world and made it ALL the way home. You will have fully become ewe, the Lamb and His Bride One at last.

Printed in the United States
By Bookmasters